## The Cricket Field
by James Pycroft

Copyright © 2019 by HardPress

Address:
HardPress
8345 NW 66TH ST #2561
MIAMI FL 33166-2626
USA
Email: info@hardpress.net

# The cricket field
James Pycroft

THE GIFT OF

HENRY GARDNER DENNY,

Of Boston, Mass.

(Class of 1852.)

Received 17 February, 1862.

## THE BOWLER,

**WILLIAM CLARKE,**

*The Slow Bowler and Sec'y to the All England Eleven.*

# THE CRICKET FIELD:

## THE HISTORY AND THE SCIENCE
## OF
## CRICKET.

BY THE AUTHOR OF
"THE PRINCIPLES OF SCIENTIFIC BATTING,"
"RECOLLECTIONS OF COLLEGE DAYS,"
ETC. ETC.

BOSTON:
W. & BAKER, WASHINGTON STREET.
1859.

# THE CRICKET FIELD:

## OR,

## THE HISTORY AND THE SCIENCE

### OF

## CRICKET.

BY THE AUTHOR OF
"THE PRINCIPLES OF SCIENTIFIC BATTING,"
"RECOLLECTIONS OF COLLEGE DAYS,"
ETC. ETC.

Gaudet ...... aprici gramine campi.—HOR.

BOSTON:
MAYHEW & BAKER, 208 WASHINGTON STREET,
1859.

SG 1315.4.5

1862, Feb. 17.
Gift of
Henry G. Denny, Es.
of Boston.
(Class of 1852)

# PREFACE

## TO THE AMERICAN EDITION.

IN nearly all the cricket manuals published in England, we find reference made to William Clarke, whose portrait we have copied from the English edition of "The Cricket Field," but can find no sketch of him. For the following we are indebted to William H. Bray, Esq., the Cricket Editor of "The New York Clipper:" "William Clarke was born at Nottingham, in 1798, and entered the cricketing arena at an early age, in which he was known as the 'Slow Bowler of Notts.' He was one of the founders, I believe, of the All England Eleven, and was, for many years, and up to the time of his death, which occurred about a year since, their Secretary. He was not a very brilliant player, but his knowledge and management of the game rendered him eligible for any eleven. His slow bowling sometimes proved very destructive to the best batsmen."

BOSTON, Sept. 22, 1859.

𝔇𝔢𝔡𝔦𝔠𝔞𝔱𝔢𝔡

TO

THE MEMBERS

OF THE

NORTH DEVON CRICKET CLUB,

BY

THEIR SINCERE FRIEND,

THE AUTHOR.

# PREFACE

## TO THE ENGLISH EDITION.

THE following pages are devoted to the history and the science of our National Game. Isaac Walton has added a charm to the Rod and Line; Col. Hawker to the Dog and the Gun; and Nimrod and Harry Hieover to the "Hunting Field;" but the "Cricket Field" is to this day untrodden ground. We have been long expecting to hear of some chronicler aided and abetted by the noblemen and gentlemen of the Marylebone Club,—one who should combine, with all the resources of a ready writer, traditionary lore and practical experience. But time is fast thinning the ranks of the veterans. Lord Frederick Beauclerk and the once celebrated player, the Hon. Henry Tufton, afterwards Earl of Thanet, have passed away; and probably Sparkes, of the Edinburgh Ground, and Mr. John Goldham, hereinafter mentioned, are the only surviving players who have witnessed both the formation and the jubilee of the Marylebone Club, following as it has the fortunes of the Pavilion and of the enterprising Thomas Lord, literally through "three removes" and "one fire," from White Conduit Fields to the present Lord's.

How, then, it will be asked, do *we* presume to save from oblivion the records of Cricket?

As regards the antiquity of the game, our history is the result of patient researches in old English literature. As regards its changes and chances and the players of olden time, it fortunately happens that, some fifteen years ago, we furnished ourselves with old Nyren's account of the cricketers of his time and the Hambledon Club, and took Bentley's Book of Matches from 1786 to 1825 to suggest questions and test the truth of answers, and passed many an interesting hour in Hampshire and Surrey by the peat fires of those villages which reared the Walkers, David Harris, Beldham, Wells, and nearly all of the All England players of fifty years since. Bennett, Harry Hampton, Beldham, and Sparkes, who first taught us to play,—all men of the last century,—have at various times contributed to our earlier annals; while Thomas Beagley, for some days our landlord, the late Mr. Ward, and especially Mr. E. H. Budd, often our antagonist in Lansdown matches, have respectively assisted in the first twenty years of the present century.

But distinct mention must we make of one most important chronicler, whose recollections were coëxtensive with the whole history of the game in its matured and perfect form—WILLIAM FENNEX. And here we must thank our kind friend, the Rev. John Mitford, of Benhall, for his memoranda of many a winter's evening with that fine old player,—papers especially valuable because Fennex's impressions were so distinct, and his observation so correct, that, added to his practical illustrations both with bat and ball, no other man could so truthfully enable us to compare ancient with modern times. Old Fennex, in his declining years, was hospitably appointed by Mr. Mitford to a sinecure office, created expressly in his honor, in the beautiful gardens of Benhall; and Pilch, and Box and Bailey, and all his old acquaintance, will not be surprised to hear that the old man would carefully water and roll his little cricket-ground on summer mornings, and on wet and wintry days would sit in the chimney-corner, dealing over and over again by the hour, to an imaginary partner, a very dark and dingy pack of cards, and would then sally forth to teach a long-remembered lesson to some hob-nailed frequenter of the village ale-house.

Some amateurs no doubt there are who could add or replace

many a link in our chain of history; and, if they will kindly come forward, we will thankfully avail ourselves of their assistance in future editions. By such collective information we may gradually build up a full and satisfactory history of our game. For the present we disdain not to offer our work to the lovers of Cricket as an outline to fill up, or as a series of pigeon-holes for general contributions.

So much for the History: but why should we venture on the Science of the game?

Many may be excellently qualified, and have a fund of anecdote and illustration, still not one of the many will venture on a book. Hundreds play without knowing principles; many know what they cannot explain; and some could explain, but fear the certain labor and cost, with the most uncertain return, of authorship. For our own part, we have felt our way. The wide circulation of our "Recollections of College Days" and "Course of English Reading" promises a patient hearing on subjects within our proper sphere; and that in this sphere lies Cricket, we may without vanity presume to assert. For, in August last, at Mr. Dark's Repository at Lord's, our little Treatise on the "Principles of Scientific Batting" (Slatter: Oxford, 1835) was singled out as "the book that contained as much on Cricket as all that had ever been written, and more besides." The same character we find given to it in Blaine's "Encyclopædia of Rural Sports." That same day did we proceed to arrange with Messrs. Longman, naturally desirous to lead a second advance movement, as we led the first, and to break the spell which we had thus been assured, had, for fifteen years, chained down the invention of literary cricketers at the identical point where we left off; for not a single rule or principle has yet been published in advance of our own; though more than one author has adopted (thinking, no doubt, the parents were dead) our ideas, and language too!

"Shall we ever make new books," asks Tristram Shandy,

"as apothecaries make new mixtures, by pouring only out of one vessel into another?"

Common modesty should have suggested to such authors the example of gipsies, who, when they steal a horse, at least pay the owner the compliment of cropping the mane and tail. And, in this, no one will suspect us of making any allusion to Mr. Felix. We could no more boast a resemblance to his book than to his play; indeed, we both play left-handed, while we write "like other folk." "Great men have the same ideas," though we wrote first; and, if "the force of *genius* could no further go," and our sails first took the wind, who could help it? And now we may run parallel without meeting, except—and we care not how often—in the cricket field; for our respective designs are now wholly different. Mr. Felix attempts but a segment: we would comprehend the whole circle. He addresses the initiated: we bend to "the meanest capacity; steering, however, a middle course, that the learner may not find us too deep, nor the learned too shallow. The plain and palatable is provided for the young people, though a few things more highly seasoned appeared only a proper compliment to the old.

Like solitary travellers from unknown lands, we are naturally desirous to offer some confirmation of statements, depending otherwise too much on our literary honor. We, happily, have received the following from—we believe the oldest player of the day that can be pronounced a good player still—Mr. E. H. Budd:—

"I return the proof sheets of the History of my Cotemporaries, and can truly say that they do indeed remind me of old times. I find one thing only to correct, which I hope you will be in time to alter, for your accuracy will then, to the best of my belief, be wholly without exception:—write *twenty* guineas, and not *twenty-five*, as the sum offered, by old Thomas Lord, if any one should hit out of his ground where now is Dorset Square.

"You invite me to note further particulars for your second

edition: the only omission I can at present detect is this,—the name of Lord George Kerr, son of the Marquis of Lothian, should be added to your list of the Patrons of the Old Surrey Players; for his lordship lived in the midst of them at Farnham, and I have often heard Beldham say, used to provide bread and cheese and beer for as many as would come out and practise on a summer's evening: this is too *substantial* a supporter of the Noble Game to be forgotten."

We must not conclude without grateful acknowledgments to some distinguished amateurs representing the science both of the northern and the southern counties, who have kindly allowed us to compare notes on various points of play. In all of our instructions in batting, we have greatly benefited by the assistance, in the first instance, of Mr. A. Bass, of Burton, and his friend Mr. Whateley, a gentleman who truly understands "Philosophy in Sport." Then the Hon. Robert Grimston judiciously suggested some modification of our plan. We agreed with him that, for a popular work, and one "for play hours," the lighter parts should prevail over the heavier, for, with most persons, a little science goes a long way, and, if made too weighty, our "winged words" might not fly far; seeing, as said Thucydides,* "men do find it such a bore to learn any thing that gives them trouble." For these reasons we drew more largely on our funds of anecdote and illustration, which had been greatly enriched by the contributions of a most valued correspondent Mr. E. S. E. Hartopp, and Mr. C. G. Merewether. Captain Cheslyn did our cause good service in other ways. When thus the science of batting had been reduced to its fair proportions, it was happily undertaken by the Hon. Frederick Ponsonby, not only through kindness to ourselves personally, but also, we feel assured, because he takes a pleasure in protecting the interests of the rising generation. By his advice we

---

* B. i. c. 20.

became more distinct in our explanations, and particularly careful of venturing on such refinements of science as, though sound in theory, may possibly produce errors in practice.

"*Tantæ molis erat* CRICETANUM *condere* CAMPUM."

For our artist we have one word to say: we allude to the illustrations of attitudes. In vain did our artist assure us that a fore-shortened position would defy every attempt at ease, energy, or elegance; and that, as a batsman looks better in any point of view than as seen by the bowler, no drawings from such a position could be satisfactory. Still, we were bound to insist on sacrificing, if necessary, the effect of the picture to its utility as an illustration. The figures, pp. 132 and 151 will prove how much more effective is a side view. Our principal design is to show the position of the feet and bat with regard to the wicket, and how every hit, with one exception, the Cut, is made by no other change of attitude than results from the movement of the left foot alone. .

J. P.

*Barnstaple,*
*April 15th,* 1851.

# CONTENTS.

### CHAP. I.
Origin of the Game of Cricket .......................... Page 13

### CHAP. II.
The General Character of Cricket ...................... 25

### CHAP. III.
The Hambledon Club and the Old Players .............. 41

### CHAP. IV.
Cricket generally established as a National Game by the end of the last Century ................................... 55

### CHAP. V.
The First Twenty Years of the present Century .......... 78

### CHAP. VI.
A dark Chapter in the History of Cricket ............... 92

### CHAP. VII.
The Science and Art of Batting ........................ 102

## CHAP. VIII.
Hints against Slow Bowling .......................... 162

## CHAP. IX.
Bowling.—An Hour with "Old Clarke" ............... 172

## CHAP. X.
Hints on Fielding..................................... 183

## CHAP. XI.
Chapter of Accidents.—Miscellaneous ................. 204

# THE CRICKET FIELD.

## CHAPTER I.

### ORIGIN OF THE GAME OF CRICKET.

The Game of Cricket, in some rude form, is undoubtedly as old as the thirteenth century. But whether at that early date Cricket was the name it generally bore is quite another question. For Club-Ball we believe to be the name which usually stood for Cricket in the thirteenth century; though, at the same time, we have some curious evidence that the term Cricket at that early period was also known. But the identity of the game with that now in use is the chief point; the name is of secondary consideration. Games commonly change their names, and, as every schoolboy knows, bear different appellations in different places.

Nevertheless, all previous writers acquiescing quietly in the opinion of Strutt, in his " Sports and Pastimes," not only forget that Cricket may be older than its name, but erroneously suppose that the name of Cricket occurs in no author in the English language earlier than Thomas D'Urfey, who, in his "Pills to purge Melancholy," writes thus:—

> "Her was the prettiest fellow
> At foot-ball and at *Cricket;*
> At hunting chase or nimble race
> *How featly* her could prick it."

The words "How featly" Strutt properly writes in place of a revolting old-fashioned oath in the original.

Strutt, therefore, in these lines, quotes the word Cricket as first occurring in 1710.

About the same date Pope wrote,—

> "The Judge to dance his brother Sergeants call,
> The Senators at *Cricket* urge the ball."

And Duncome laying, curious to observe, the scene of a match near Canterbury, wrote,—

> "An ill-timed *Cricket Match* there did
> At Bishops-bourne befal."

Soame Jenyns, also, early in the same century, wrote in lines that showed that cricket was very much of a "sporting" amusement:—

> "England, when once of peace and wealth possessed,
> Began to think frugality a jest;
> So grew polite: hence all her well-bred heirs
> Gamesters and jockeys turned, and cricket-players."
>                                   Ep. I. b. ii., *init.*

However, we are happy to say that even among comparatively modern authors we have beaten Strutt in his researches by twenty-five years; for Edward Phillips, John Milton's nephew, in his "Mysteries of Love and Eloquence," (8vo. 1685), writes thus:—

"Will you not, when you have me, throw stocks at my head and cry, 'Would my eyes had been beaten out of my head with a *cricket-ball* the day before I saw thee?'"

A late author has very sensibly remarked that the game could not have been popular in the days of Elizabeth, or we should expect to find allusions to cricket, as to tennis, football, and other sports, in the early poets; but, he says, Shakspeare and the dramatists who followed are silent on the subject.

The silence of the early poets and dramatists as to the game of cricket — and no one conversant with English literature would expect to find it except in some casual allusion or illustration in an old play — we can confirm on the best authority. It would seem bold to say that the early dramatists are, one and all, silent on the game of cricket. How bold a negative! So rare are certain old plays that a hundred pounds have been paid by the Duke of Devonshire for a single play of a few loose and soiled leaves; and shall we pretend to have dived among such hidden stores? We are so fortunate as to be favored with the assistance of the Rev. John Milford and our loving cousin John

Payne Collier, two English scholars, most deeply versed in early literature, and no bad judges of cricket; and since these two scholars have never met with any mention of cricket in the early dramatists, nor in any author earlier than 1685, there is, indeed, much reason to believe that "Cricket" is a word that does not occur in any English author before 1685.

But though not in any English author, does it occur in no document yet unpublished? We shall see.

Now as regards the silence of the early poets, a game like cricket might certainly exist without falling in with the descriptions or topics of those writers. But if we actually find distinct catalogues and enumerations of English games before the date of 1685, and cricket still omitted, the suspicion that cricket was not then the popular name of one of the many games of ball (not that the game was itself unknown) is strongly confirmed.

Three such catalogues do occur; one in the "Anatomy of Melancholy," a second in a well-known treatise of James I., and a third in the "Cotswold Games."

For the first catalogue, Strutt reminds us of the set of rules from the hand of James I. for the "nurture and conduct of an heir-apparent to the throne," addressed to his eldest son, Henry Prince of Wales, called the ΒΑΣΙΛΙΚΟΝ ΔΩΡΟΝ, or a "Kinge's Christian Dutie towards God." Herein the king forbids gaming and rough play: "As to diceing, I think it becometh best deboshed souldiers to play on the heads of their drums. As to the foote-ball, it is meeter for laming than making able the users thereof." But a special commendation is given to certain games of ball; " playing at the catch or tennis, palle-malle, and *such like other* fair and pleasant *field-games."* Certainly cricket may have been included under the last general expression, though by no means a fashionable game in James's reign.

For the second catalogue of games, Burton, in his " Anatomy of Melancholy," " the only book," said Dr. Johnson, " that ever took me out of bed two hours sooner than I wished to rise,"— gives a view of the sports most prevalent in the seventeenth century. Here we have a very full enumeration: it specifies the pastimes of " great men," and those of " base, inferior persons ;" it mentions " the rocks on which men lose themselves " by gambling; how " wealth runs away with their hounds, and their fortunes fly away with their hawks." Then follow " the sights and shows of the Londoners," and the " May-games and recreations of the country folk." More minutely still, Burton speaks of rope-dancers, cock-fights, and other sports common both to town and country; and though he is so exact as to specify all " winter recreations " separately, and mentions " foot-balls and ballowns," and says, " Let the common people play at ball and barley-brakes," still is there, in all this catalogue, no mention of cricket.

As a third catalogue we have the "Cotswold Games," but cricket is not among them. This was an annual celebration which one Captain Dover, by express permission and command of James I., held on the Cotswold Hills, in Gloucestershire.

Fourthly : cricket is not mentioned in "The Compleat Gamester," published by Charles Browne, in 1709.

But we have a catalogue of games about the same date, in Stow's "Survey of London," there cricket is mentioned ; but, remarkably enough, it is particularized as one of the amusements of "the lower classes." The whole passage is curious : —

"The modern sports of the citizens, *besides drinking* (!), are cock-fighting, bowling upon greens, backgammon, cards, dice, billiards, also musical entertainments, dancing, masks, balls, stage-plays, and club-meetings in the evening; they sometimes ride out on horseback, and hunt with the lord mayor's pack of dogs, when the common hunt goes on. The *lower classes* divert themselves at foot-ball, wrestling, cudgels, ninepins, shovel-board, *cricket*, stow-ball, ringing of bells, quoits, pitching the bar, bull and bear baitings, throwing at cocks, and lying at ale-houses." (!)

The mention of one thing is the negation of the other, say the lawyers; and this rule of evidence certainly applies to an omission from three distinct catalogues, and the conclusion that cricket was unknown when those lists were made would appear inevitable, were it not that in this case the argument would prove too much; for it would equally prove that club-ball and trap-ball were undiscovered too; whereas both these games are as old as the thirteenth century.

The conclusion of all this is, that the oft-repeated assertions that cricket is a game no older than the eighteenth century is erroneous; for, first, the game itself may be much older than the name by which we know it; and, secondly, the "silence of antiquity" is no conclusive evidence that even the name, Cricket, was really unknown.

Thus do we refute those who assert a negative as to the antiquity of cricket. Next, for our affirmative, we will show —

First, that the game of single-wicket was played as early as the thirteenth century, under the name of Club-ball.

Secondly, that it might have been played at the same time as "Handyn and Handoute."

Thirdly, that the genuine double-wicket game was played in Scotland about 1700, under the name of " Cat and Dog."

Fourthly, that "Creag,"—very near "Cricce," the Saxon term for the crooked stick, or bandy, which we see in the old pictures of cricket,—was the name of a game played in the year 1300.

First, as to a single-wicket game in the thirteenth

century, whatever the name of the said game might have been, we are quite satisfied with the following proof:—

"In the Bodleian Library at Oxford," says Strutt, "is a MS. (No. 264,) dated 1344, which represents a figure, a female, in the act of bowling a ball (of the size of a modern cricket-ball) to a man who elevates a straight bat to strike it; behind the bowler are several figures, male and female, waiting to stop or catch the ball, their attitudes grotesquely eager for a 'chance.' The game is called club-ball, but the score is made by hitting and running, as in cricket."

Secondly, Barrington, in his remarks on the more ancient statutes, comments on 17 Edw. IV. A. D. 1477, thus:—

"The disciplined soldiers were not only guilty of pilfering on their return, but also of the vice of gaming. The third chapter therefore forbids playing at cloish, ragle, half-bowle, quekebord, *handyn and handoute.* Whosoever shall permit these games to be played in their house or yard is punishable with three years' imprisonment; those who play at any of the said games are to be fined 10*l.*, or lie in jail two years.

"This," says Barrington, "is the most severe law ever made in any country against gaming, and some of those forbidden seem to have been manly exercises, particularly the handyn and handoute, which I should suppose to be a kind of *cricket,* as the term *hands* is still (writing in 1740) retained in that game."

Thirdly, as to the double-wicket game, Dr. Jamieson, in his Dictionary, published in 1722, gives the following account of a game played in Angus and Lothian:—

"This is a game for three players at least, who are furnished with clubs. They cut out two holes, each about a foot in diameter and seven inches in depth, and twenty-six feet apart; one man guards each hole with his club; these clubs are called Dogs. A piece of wood, about four inches long and one inch in diameter, called a cat, is pitched, by a third person, from one hole towards the player at the other, who is to prevent the cat from getting into the hole. If it pitches in the hole, the party who threw it takes his turn with the club. If the cat be struck, the club-bearers change places, and each change of place counts one to the score, *like club ball*."

The last observation shows that in the game of club-ball above-mentioned, the score was made by "runs," as in cricket.

In what respect, then, do these games differ from cricket, as played now? The only exception that can be taken is to the absence of any wicket. But every one familiar with a paper given by Mr. Ward, and published in "Old Nyren," by the talented Mr. C. Cowden Clarke, — a friend of Charles Lamb, and his style has a genuine savour of "Elia,"— will remember that the traditionary "blockhole" was a veritable hole in former times, and that the batsman was made out in running, not, as now, but putting down a wicket, but by popping the ball into the hole before the bat was grounded in it. The same paper represents that the wicket was two feet wide,— a width which is only rendered credible by the fact that the said hole was not like our mark for guard, four feet distant from the stumps, but between them; an arrangement which would require space for the frequent struggle of the batsman and wicket-keeper, as to who should reach the blockhole first.

The conclusion of all is, that cricket is identical with club-ball,— a game played in the thirteenth century as single-wicket, and played, if not then, later as a double-wicket game; that where balls were scarce, a Cat, or bit of wood, as seen in many a village, supplied its place; also that handyn and handoute was probably another name. Fosbroke, in his Dictionary of Antiquities, said " club-ball was the ancestor of cricket: " he might have said, " club-ball was the old name for cricket, the games being the same."

The points of difference are not greater than every cricketer can show between the game as now played and that of the last century.

But, lastly, as to the name of cricket. The bat, which is now straight, is represented in old pictures as crooked, and " cricce " is the simple Saxon word for a crooked stick. The derivation of billiards from the Norman *billart*, a cue, or from ball-yard, according to Johnson, also ninepins and trapball, are obvious instances of games which derived their names from the implements with which they are played. Now it appears highly probable, that when a wicket to be bowled down by a rolling ball superseded the blockhole to be pitched into, that the club best suited for a pitch should have given way to the bandy or crooked bat of the last century; and, if so, the game, which first was named from the club " club-ball," should afterwards be named from the crooked stick " cricket."

Add to which the game might have been played in two ways,— sometimes more in the form of club-ball, sometimes more like cricket; and the following remarkable passage proves that a term very similar to cricket was applied to some game as far back as the thirteenth century, the identical date to which we have traced that form of cricket called club-ball and the game of handyn and handoute.

From the Gentleman's Magazine, vol. lviii. p. 1., A. D. 1788, we extract the following : —

" In the wardrobe account of the 28th year of King Edward the First, A. D. 1300, published in 1787 by the Society of Antiquaries, among the entries of money paid his chaplain, one Mr. John Leek, for the use of his son Prince Edward in playing at different games, is the following : —

"' Domino Johanni de Leek, capellano Domini Edwardi fil' ad *Creag'* et alios ludos per vices, per manus proprias, 100 s. Apud Westm. 10 die Aprilis, 1305.' "

The writer observes, that the glossaries have been searched in vain for any other name of a pastime but cricket to which the term Creag' can apply.

Creag' and cricket, therefore, being presumed identical, the cricketers of Warwick and of Gloucester may be reminded that they are playing the same game as was played by the dauntless enemy of Robert Bruce, afterwards the prisoner at Kenilworth, and lastly the victim of Mortimer's ruffians in the dark tragedy of Berkeley Castle.

The same game in later times, we know, has been the pastime and discipline of many an English soldier. Our barracks are now provided with cricket grounds; every regiment and every man-of-war has its club; and our soldiers and sailors astonish the natives of every clime, both inland and maritime, with a specimen of a British game: and it deserves to be better known that it was at a cricket match that "some of our officers were amusing themselves on the 12th June, 1815," says Captain Gordon, "in company with that devoted cricketer, the Duke of Richmond, when the Duke of Wellington arrived, and shortly after came the Prince of Orange, which of course put a stop to our game. Though the hero of the Peninsula was not apt to let his movements be known, on this occasion he made no secret that, if he were attacked from the south, Halle would be his position, and, if on the Namur side, WATERLOO."

## CHAP. II.

#### THE GENERAL CHARACTER OF CRICKET.

THE game of cricket, philosophically considered, is a standing panegyric on the English character; none but an orderly and sensible race of people would so amuse themselves. It calls into requisition all the cardinal virtues, some moralist would say. As with the Grecian games of old, the player must be sober and temperate. Patience, fortitude, and self-denial, the various bumps of order, obedience, and good humour, with an unruffled temper, are indispensable. For intellectual virtues we want judgment, decision, and the organ of concentrativeness — every faculty in the free use of all its limbs — and every idea in constant air and exercise. Poor, rickety, and stunted wits will never serve: the widest shoulders are of little use without a head upon them: the cricketer wants wits down to his fingers' ends. As to physical qualifications, we require not only the volatile spirits of the Irishman *Rampant*, nor the phlegmatic caution of the Scotchman *Couchant*, but we want the English combination of the two; though, with good generalship, cricket is a game for Britons generally: the three nations would mix not better in a regiment than an eleven; especially if the Hibernian were trained in London, and taught to enjoy something better than what has been termed his supreme felicity, "Otium cum dig-*gin-taties*." From the southern and south-eastern counties of England the game spread — not a little owing to the Propaganda of the metropolitan clubs, which played chiefly first at the Artillery Ground, then at White Conduit Fields, and lastly at Lord's, as well as latterly at the Oval, Kennington, and on all sides of London — through all the southern half of England; and during these last twenty years the northern counties, and even Edinburgh, have sent forth distinguished players. But considering that the complement of the game is twenty-two men, besides two umpires and two scorers; and considering also that cricket, unlike every other manly contest, by flood or field, occupies commonly more than one day; the railways, as might be expected, have tended wonderfully to the diffusion of cricket, — giving rise to clubs depending on a circle of some thirty or forty miles, as also to that club in particular under the canonized saint, John Zingari, into whom are supposed to have migrated all the erratic spirits of the gipsy tribe. The Zingari are a race of ubiquitous cricketers, exclusively gentlemen-players; for cricket affords to a race of professionals a merry and abundant, though rather a laborious livelihood, from the time that the May-fly is up to the time the first pheasant is down. Neither must we forget the All England Eleven, who, under the generalship of Mr. Clarke of Nottingham, play numbers varying from sixteen to twenty-two in almost every country in England; and so proud are the clubs of the honour that, besides a subscription of some 70*l.*, and part or all of the money at the field-gate, being willingly accorded for their services, much hospitality is exercised wherever they go. This tends to a healthy circulation of the life's blood of cricket, vaccinating and inoculating every wondering rustic with the principles of the national game. Our soldiers, we said, by order of the Horse Guards, are provided with cricket-grounds adjoining their barracks; and all of her Majesty's ships have bats and balls to astonish the cockroaches at sea, and the crabs and turtles ashore. Hence it has come to pass that, wherever her Majesty's servants have "carried their victorious arms" and legs, wind and weather permitting, cricket has been played. Still the game is essentially Anglo-Saxon. Foreigners have rarely, very rarely, imitated us. The English settlers and residents everywhere play; but of no single cricket club have we ever heard dieted either with frogs, sour crout, or macaroni. But how remarkable that cricket is not naturalized in Ireland! the fact is very striking that it follows the course rather of ale than whiskey. Witness Kent, the land of hops, and the annual antagonists of "All England." Secondly, Parnham, which, as we shall presently show, with its adjoining parishes, nurtured the finest of the old players, as well as the finest hops,— *cunabula Trojæ*, the infant school of cricketers. Witness also the Burton Clubs, assisted by our excellent friend next akin to bitter ale. Witness again Alton ale, on which old Beagley throve so well, and the Scotch ale of Edinburgh, on which John Sparkes, though commencing with the last generation, has carried on his instructions, in which we ourselves once rejoiced, into the middle of the present century. The mountain mists and "mountain dew" suit better with deer stalking than with cricket: our game disdains the Dutch courage of ardent spirits. The brain must glow with nature's fire, and not depend upon a spirit lamp. *Mens sana in corpore sano*: feed the body, but do not cloud the mind. You, sir, with the hectic flush, the fire of your eyes burnt low in their sockets, with beak as sharp as a woodcock's from living upon suction, with pallid face and shaky hand,—our game disdains such ghostlike votaries. Rise with the lark and scent the morning air, and drink from the bubbling rill, and then, when your veins are no longer fevered with alcohol, nor puffed with tobacco smoke,—when you have rectified your illicit spirits and clarified your unsettled judgment,—"come again and devour up my discourse." And you, sir, with the figure of Falstaff and the nose of Bardolf,—not Christianly eating that you may live, but living that you may eat,—one of the *nati consumere fruges*, the devouring caterpillar and grub of human kind: our noble game has no sympathy with gluttony, still less with the habitual " diner-out," on whom outraged nature has taken vengeance, by emblazoning what was his face (*nimium ne crede colori,*) encasing each limb in fat, and condemning him to be his own porter to the end of his days. " Then I am your man—and I—and I," cry a crowd of self-satisfied youths; " sound are we in wind and limb, and none have quicker hand or eye." Gently, my friends, so far well; good hands and eyes are instruments indispensable, but only instruments. There is a wide difference between a good workman and a bag of tools, however sharp. We must have head as well as hands. You may be big enough and strong enough, but the question is whether, as Virgil says,

" *Spiritus intus alit, totamque infusa per artus
Mens agitat molem, et magno se corpore miscet.*"

And in these lines Virgil truly describes the right sort of man for a cricketer: plenty of life in him: not barely soul enough, as Robert South said, to keep his body from putrefaction; but, however large his stature, though he weigh twenty stone, like (we will not say Mr. Mynn), but an olden wicket-keeper, named Burt, or a certain *infant* genius in the same line, of good

Cambridge town,—he must, like these worthies aforesaid, have *nous* in perfection, and be instinct with sense all over. Then, says Virgil, *igneus est ollis vigor;* " they must always have the steam up," otherwise the bard would have agreed with us, they are no good in an Eleven, because—

" *Noxia corpora tardant*
*Terrenique hebetant artus, moribundaque membra;* "

that is, you must suspend the laws of gravitation before they can stir,—dull clods of the valley, and so many stone of carrion; and then Virgil proceeds to describe the discipline to render those who suffer the penalties of idleness or intemperance fit to join the chosen *few* in the cricket-field:

" *Exinde per amplum*
*Mittimur Elysium et pauci læta arva tenemus.*"

Superfluous were it to make any apology for classical quotations; above all when the English is appended. At the Universities, cricket and scholarship very generally go together. When, in 1836, we played victoriously on the side of Oxford against Cambridge, seven out of our eleven were classmen, and it is doubtless only to avoid an invidious distinction that " Heads *v.* Heels," as was once suggested, has failed to be an annual University match; the *seri studiorum* —those put to school late—would not have a chance. From all this we argue that, on the authority of ancient and the experience of modern times, cricket was mind as well as matter, and, in every sense of the word, a good understanding. How is it that Clarke's slow bowling is so successful? Ask Bayley or Caldecourt; or say Bayley's own bowling, or that of Lillywhite, or others not much indebted to pace. "You see, sir, they bowl with their heads." Then only is the game worthy the notice of full-grown men. "A rubber of whist," says the author of the "Diary of a Late Physician," in his "Law Studies," "calls into requisition all those powers of mind that a barrister most needs;" and nearly as much may be said of a scientific game of cricket. Mark that first-rate bowler; the batsman is hankering for his favorite cut—no—leg stump is attacked again—extra man on leg side—right —that's the spot—leg stump, and not too near him. He is screwed up, and cannot cut away; Point has it —persevere—try again—his patience soon will fail. Ah, look at that ball; the bat was more out of the perpendicular—now the bowler alters his pace—good. A dropping ball—over-reached and all but a mistake; now a slower pace still, with extra twist—hits furiously to leg, too soon. Leg-stump is grazed, and bail off. "You see, sir," says the veteran, turning round, "a man has no room to cut from leg-stump—is more apt to hit across from leg-stump—is often caught from leg-stump; even "leg before wicket" comes from leg-stump—gets off his ground from leg-stump, and cannot stop so readily from leg-stump—so keep on at leg-stump with an imperfect player. It wants a very long-headed player; aye, and one of steady habits, the result of long experience in all the chances of the game, to remain steady ball after ball. An old player, who knows what is and what is not on the ball, alone can resist all the temptations that leg-balls involve. Young players are going their round of experiments, and are too fond of admiration and brilliant hits; whereas it is your upright straight players that worry a bowler—twenty-two inches of wood, by four and a quarter—every inch of them before the stumps, hitting or blocking, is ra-ther disheartening; but the moment a man makes ready for a leg hit, the bat points to Slip instead of to bails, and only about five inches by four of wood can cover the wicket; so leg-hitting is the bowler's chance: cutting also for a similar reason. If there were no such thing as leg-hitting, we should see a full bat every time, the man steady on his legs, and only one thing to think of; and what a task a bowler would have. That was Mr. Ward's play—good for something to the last. First-rate straight play and free leg-hitting seldom last long together: when once exulting in the luxurious excitement of a leg-volley, the muscles are always on the quiver to swipe round, and the bowler sees the bat raised more and more across wicket. So, also, it is with men who are yearning for a cut—forming for the cut like forming for leg-hit, aye, and almost the idea of those hits coming across the mind, set the muscles off straight play, and give the bowler a chance. There is a deal of headwork in bowling: once make your batsman set his mind on one hit, and give him a ball requiring the contrary, and he is off his guard in a moment."

"Lillywhite," said a first-rate Cambridge mathematician and cricketer who knew him well, "has a mind that would have made him eminent in many positions in life. The game, when he plays it, is very often the bowler's head and hands against the batman's hands alone. Of course, the old professional players at last have learnt all his manœuvres: but then it is no small praise to him that they have had to learn it; and he has raised the standard of batting, and remained a first-rate bowler nearly half a century. It will easily be understood, therefore, that there is something highly intellectual in our noble and national pastime. But the cricketer must possess certain qualifications, not only physical and intellectual, but moral qualifications also; but of what avail is the mind to design, and the hand to execute, if a sulky temper paralyzes his exertions, and throws a damp upon the field; or if impatience dethrones judgment, and the man hits across at good balls, because loose balls are long in coming; or, again, if a contentious and imperious disposition leaves the cricketer all 'alone in his glory,' voted the pest of every eleven."

The pest of the hunting-field is the man always thinking of his own horse and own riding, galloping against MEN and not after DOGS. The pest of the cricket-field is the man who bores you about his average—his wickets—his catches; and looks blue, even at the success of his own party. If unsuccessful in batting or fielding, he "shuts up"—"the wretch concentred all in self." No! Give me the man who forgets himself in the game, and, missing a ball, does not stop to exculpate himself by dumb show, but rattles away after it—who does not blame his partner when he is run out—who plays like play, and not like earnest—who can say good-humoredly, "runs enough I hope without mine." If such a man makes a score, players remark on all sides, "Our friend deserves luck for his good-humor and true spirit of the game."

Add to all this, perseverance and self-denial, and a soul above vain glory and the applause of the vulgar. Aye, perseverance in well-doing,—perseverance in a straight-forward, upright and consistent course of action.—See that player practising apart from the rest. What an unpretending style of play—a hundred pounds appears to depend on every ball—not a hit for these five minutes—see, he has a shilling on his stumps, and Hillyer is doing his best to knock it off. A question asked after every ball, the bowler being constantly invited to remind him of the least inaccuracy in hitting or danger in defence. The other players are hitting all over the field, making every one (but a good judge) marvel. Our friend's reward is that in the first good match, when some supposed brilliant Mr. Dashwood has been stumped from leg ball—(he cannot make his fine hits in his ground)—bowled by a shooter or caught by that sharpest of all Points, "ἴναξ ἀνδρῶν see our persevering friend—ball after ball dropping harmless from his bat, till ever and anon a single or a double are safely played away—two figures are appended to his name; and Caldecourt, as he puts the bails on, remarks, " We've some good cricket this morning, gentlemen."

Conceit in a cricketer, as in other things, is a bar to all improvement—the vain-glorious is always thinking of the lookers-on instead of the game, and generally is condemned to live on the reputation of one skying leg-hit, or some twenty runs off three or four overs (his merriest life is a short one) for half a season.

In one word, there is no game in which amiability and an unruffled temper is so essential to success, or in which virtue is rewarded half as much as in the game of cricket. Dishonest or shuffling ways cannot prosper; the umpires will foil every such attempt—those truly constitutional judges, bound by a code of written laws—and the public opinion of a cricket club, militates against his preferment. For cricket is a social game. Could a cricketer play a solo, or with a dummy (other than the catapult), he might play in humor or out of humor; but an Eleven is of the nature of those commonwealths of which Cicero said, that without some regard to the cardinal virtues, they could not possibly hold together.

The game of cricket—would that all men would remember!—is truly a game—a recreation; so away with pettish words and sombre looks. "If it's play, why look so serious and unhappy?" said a lady once in our hearing; and added, with that fine discernment in which ladies so much excel, "cricket never appears to me so honestly a game of play as when Mr. Charles Taylor holds the bat—every movement is so easy, the whole field is made alive, and his style and appearance so joyous."

Cricket is not solely a game of skill—chance has sway enough to leave the vanquished an *if* and a *but*. A long innings bespeaks good play; but "out the first ball" is no disgrace. A game, to be really a game, really playful, should admit of chance as well as skill. It is the bane of chess that its character is too severe.—to lose its games is to lose your character; and, most painful of all, to be outwitted in a fair and undeniable contest of long-headedness, tact, manœuvring, and common sense—qualities in which no man likes to come off second best. There stand the same mechanical pieces alike for both: the sole difference consists in the mind of the player. Hence the restless nights and unforgiving state of mind that has so often followed one checkmate. Hence that "agony of rage and disappointment from which," said Sydney Smith, "the Bishop of ——— broke my head with a chess-board fifty years ago at college."

But did we say that ladies, famed as some have been in the hunting-field, know anything of cricket too? Not often; though I could have mentioned two,—the wife and daughter of the late William Ward, all three now no more, who could tell you,—the daughter especially—the forte and the failing of every player at Lord's. I accompanied them home one evening to see some records of the game, to their humble abode in Connaught Terrace, where many an ornament reminded me of the former magnificence of the Member for the City, the Bank Director, and the great Russia merchant, when in his mansion in the then not unfashionable Bloomsbury Square, the banqueting room of which many a Wykehamist has cause to remember; for when famed, as they were, for the quickest and best of fielding, the Wykehamists had won their annual match at Lord's, and twenty years since they but rarely lost, Mr. Ward would bear away triumphantly the winners to end the day with him. But talking of the ladies, to say nothing of Miss Wills, who invented over-hand bowling, their natural powers of criticism, if honestly consulted, would, we think, tell some home truths to a certain class of players who seem to forget that to be a cricketer he must be still a man; and that a manly, graceful style of play is worth something, independently of effect on the score. Take the case of the Skating Club. Will they elect a man because, in spite of arms and legs centrifugally flying, he can do some tricks of a posture-master, however wonderful? No! elegance in simple movements is the first thing: without elegance nothing counts. And so should it be with cricket. I have seen men, accounted players, quite as bad as some of the cricketers in Mr. Pips's diary. "Pray, Lovell," I once heard, "have I the right guard?" "Guard indeed! Yes! keep on looking as ugly and as awkward as you are now, and no man in England can bowl for fright!" *Apropos*, one of the first hints in archery is, "don't make faces when you pull your bow." Now we do seriously entreat those young ladies into whose hands this book may fall to profess, on our authority, that they are judges of the game as far as appearance goes; and also that they will quiz, banter, tease, lecture, never-leave-alone, and otherwise plague and worry all such brothers or husbands as they shall see enacting these anatomical contortions, which too often disgrace the game of cricket.

Cricket, we said, is a game chiefly of skill, but partly of chance. Skill avails enough for interest, and not too much for friendly feeling. No game is played in better humor—never lost till won—the game's alive till the last ball. True it is that certain evil-disposed persons will sometimes leave all proper feelings behind them; and, if conceited of their own play, or bent on mortifying their adversaries, " angry passions rise," none can wonder. But for the most part there is so little to ruffle the temper, or to cause unpleasant collision, that there is no place so free from temptation—no such happy plains or lands of innocence—as our cricket fields. We give bail for our good behavior from the moment that we enter them. Still is a cricket-field a sphere of wholesome discipline in obedience and good order; not to mention that manly spirit that faces danger without shrinking, and bears disappointment with good nature. Disappointment! and say where is there more poignant disappointment, while it lasts, than after all your practice for a match, and anxious thought and resolution to avoid every chance, and score off every possible ball, to be balked and run out, caught at the slip, or stumped even off a shooter. "The course of true love (even for cricket) never did run smooth." Old Robinson, one of the finest batsmen of his day, had six unlucky innings in succession; once caught by Hammond, from a draw; then bowled with shooters, or picked up at short slip, the poor fellow said he had lost all his play, thinking " the fault is in ourselves, and not our stars;" and was with difficulty persuaded to play one match more, in which—whose heart does not rejoice to hear?—he made one hundred and thirty runs.

"But as to stirring excitement," writes a friend, " what can surpass a hardly contested match when you have been manfully playing an up-hill game, and gradually the figures on the telegraph keep telling a better and a better tale, till at last the scorers stand up and proclaim a tie, and you win the game by a single and rather a nervous wicket, or by five or ten runs." If in the field with a match of this sort, and trying hard to prevent these few runs being knocked off by the last wickets, I know of no excitement so intense for the time, or which lasts so long afterwards. The recollection of these critical moments will make the heart jump for years and years to come; and it is extraordinary to see the delight with which men call up these grand moments to memory; and to be sure *how* they will talk and chatter, their eyes glistening and pulses getting quicker, as if they were again finishing " that rattling good match." People talk of the excitement of a good run with the Quorn or Belvoir hunt. I have now and then tumbled in for these good things; and, as far as my own feelings go, I can safely say that a fine run is not to be compared to a good match; and the excitement of the keenest sportsman is nothing either in intensity or duration to that caused by a " near thing " at cricket. The next good run takes the place of the other; whereas hard matches, like the snow-ball, gather as they go. " This is my decided opinion; and that, after watching and weighing the subject for some years. I have seen men tremble and turn pale at a near match, while through the field the deepest and most awful silence reigns, unbroken but by some nervous fieldsman humming a tune, or snapping his fingers, to hide his agitation."

## CHAP. III.

#### THE HAMBLETON CLUB AND THE OLD PLAYERS.

What have become of the old scores and the earliest records of the game of cricket? Bentley's Book of Matches gives the principal games from the year 1786; but where are the earlier records of matches made by Dehany, Paulett, and Sir Horace Mann? All burnt!

What the destruction of Rome and its records by the Gauls was to Niebuhr,—what the fire of London was to the antiquary in his walk from Pudding Lane to Pie Corner, such was the burning of the Pavilion at Lord's, and all the old score books—it is a mercy that the old painting of the M. C. C. was saved—to the annalist of cricket. " When we were built out by Dorset Square," says Mr. E. H. Budd, " we played for three years where the Regent's Canal has since been cut, and still called our ground " Lord's," and our dining-room " the Pavilion." Here many a time have I looked over the old papers of Dehany and Sir H. Mann; but the room was burnt, and the old scores perished in the flames.

The following are curious as the oldest scores preserved,—one of the north, the other of the South: —

### NAMES OF THE PERSONS WHO PLAYED AGAINST SHEFFIELD.

In 1771 at NOTTINGHAM, and 1772 at SHEFIELD.

Nottingham, Aug. 26, 1771.
    Huthwayte
    Turner
    Loughman
    Coleman
    Roe
    Spurr
    Stocks
    Collishaw
    Troop
    Mew
    Rawson.

| Sheffield. | | Nottingham. | |
|---|---|---|---|
| 1st inn. | 81 | 1st inn. | 76 |
| 2nd | 62 | 2nd | 112 |
| 3rd | 105 | | |
| | 248 | | 188 |

Tuesday, 9 o'clock, a. m. commenced, 8th man 0, 9th 5, 1 to come in, and only 60 a head, when the Sheffield left the field.

Sheffield June 1, 1772.
    Coleman
    Turner
    Loughman
    Roe
    Spurs
    Stocks
    Collishaw
    Troop
    Mew
    Bamford
    Gladwin.

| Nottingham. | | Sheffield. |
|---|---|---|
| 1st inn. | 14 | Near 70 |

Nottingham gave in.

## KENT AGAINST ALL ENGLAND.

*Played in the Artillery-Ground, London, 1746.*

### ENGLAND.

|  | 1st Innings. RUNS. |  |  | 2nd Innings. RUNS. |  |
|---|---|---|---|---|---|
| Harris | 0 | b by Hadswell | 4 | b by | Mills. |
| Dingate | 3 | b Ditto.... | 11 | b | Hadswell. |
| Newland | 0 | b Mills .... | 3 | b | Ditto. |
| Cuddy | 0 | b Hadswell. | 2 | b | Danes. |
| Green | 0 | b Mills .... | 5 | b | Mills. |
| Waymark | 7 | b Ditto .... | 9 | b | Hadswell. |
| Bryan | 12 | s Kips .... | 7 | c | Kips. |
| Newland | 18 | — not out .. | 15 | c | Ld. J. Sackville. |
| Harris | 0 | b Hadswell. | 1 | b | Hadswell. |
| Smith | 0 | c Bartrum.. | 8 | b | Mills. |
| Newland | 0 | b Mills .... | 5 | — | not out. |
| Byes | 0 |  | 0 |  |  |
|  | **40** |  | **70** |  |  |

### KENT.

|  | 1st Innings. RUNS. |  |  | 2nd Innings. RUNS. |  |
|---|---|---|---|---|---|
| Lord Sackville | 5 | c by Waymark . | 3 | b by | Harris. |
| Long Robin | 7 | b Newland.. | 9 | b | Newland. |
| Mills | 0 | b Harris .... | 6 | c | Ditto. |
| Hadswell | 0 | b Ditto ..... | 5 | — | not out. |
| Cutbush | 3 | c Green .... | 7 | — | not out. |
| Bartrum | 2 | b Newland.. | 0 | b | Newland. |
| Danes | 6 | b Ditto ..... | 0 | c | Smith. |
| Sawyer | 0 | c Waymark . | 5 | b | Newland. |
| Kips | 12 | b Harris .... | 10 | b | Harris. |
| Mills | 7 | — not out ... | 2 | b | Newland. |
| Romney | 11 | b Harris. ... | 8 | c | Harris. |
| Byes | 0 |  | 3 |  |  |
|  | **53** |  | **58** |  |  |

And now the oldest chronicler is Old Nyren, who wrote an account of the cricketers of his time. The said Old Nyren borrowed the pen of our kind friend Charles Cowden Clarke, to whom John Keats dedicated an epistle, and who rejoiced in the friendship of Charles Lamb; and none but a kindred spirit to Elia could have written like " Old Nyren." Nyren was a fine old English yeoman, whose chivalry was cricket; and Mr. Clarke has faithfully recorded his vivid descriptions and animated recollections. And, with his charming little volume in hand, and inkhorn at my button, in 1837 I made a tour among the cottages of William Belden, and the few surviving worthies of the same generation; and, having also the advantage of a MS. by the Rev. John Midford, taken from many a winter's evening with Old Fennex, I am happy to attempt the best account that the lapse of time admits, of cricket in the olden time.

From a MS. my friend received from the late Mr. William Ward, it appears that the wickets were placed twenty-two yards apart as long since as the year 1700; that stumps were then only one foot high, but two feet wide. The width some persons have doubted; but it is rendered credible by the auxiliary evidence that there was, in those days, width enough between the two stumps for cutting the wide blockhole already mentioned, and also because—whereas now we hear of stumps and bails—we read formerly of " two stumps with one stump laid across."

We are informed, also, that putting down the wickets to make a man out in running, instead of the old custom of popping the ball into the hole, was adopted on account of severe injuries to the hands, and that the wicket was changed at the same time—1779-1780—to the dimensions of twenty-two inches by six, with a third stump added.

Before this alteration the art of defence was almost unkown : balls often passed over the wicket, and often passed through. At the time of the alteration Old Nyren truly predicted that the innings would not be shortened but better played. The long pod and curved form of the bat, as seen in the old paintings, was made only for hitting, and for ground balls too. Length balls were then by no means common; neither would low stumps encourage them : and even upright play was then practised by very few. Old Nyren relates that one Harry Hall, a gingerbread baker of Farnham, gave peripatetic lectures to young players, and always insisted on keeping the left elbow well up; in other words, on straight play. "Now-a-days," said Beldham, "all the world knows that; but when I began there was very little length bowling, very little straight play, and little defence either." Fennex, said he, was the first who played out at balls; before his day batting was too much about the crease. Beldham said that his own supposed tempting of Providence consisted in running in to hit. "You do frighten me there jumping out of your ground," said our Squire Paulett: and Fennex used also to relate how, when he played forward to the pitch of the ball, his father " had never seen the like in all his days ; " the said days extending a long way back towards the beginning of the century. While speaking of going in to hit, Beldham said, " My opinion has always been that too little is attempted in that direction. Judge your ball, and, when the least overpitched, go in and hit her away." In this opinion Mr. C. Taylor's practice would have borne Beldham out, and a fine dashing game this makes, only it is a game for none but practised players. When you are perfect in your ground, then, and then only, try what you can do out of it, as the best means to scatter the enemy and open the field.

" As to bowling," continued Beldham, " when I way a boy (say 1780), nearly all bowling was fast, and all along the ground. In those days the Hambledon Club could beat all England ; but our three parishes around Farnham beat Hambledon."

It is quite evident that Farnham was the cradle of cricketers. " Surrey," in the old scores, means nothing more than the Farnham parishes. This corner of Surrey, in every match against All England, was reckoned as part of Hampshire, and Beldham truly said " you find us regularly on the Hampshire side in Bentley's Book."

" I told you, sir," said Beldham, " that in my early

days all bowling was what we called fast, or at least a moderate pace. The first lobbing slow bowler I ever saw was Tom Walker. When, in 1792, England played Kent, I did feel so ashamed of such baby bowling; but, after all, he did more than even David Harris himself. Two years after, in 1794, at Dartford Brent, Tom Walker, with his slow bowling, headed a side against David Harris, and beat him easily."

" Kent, in early times, was not equal to our counties. Their great man was Crawte, and he was taken away from our parish of Alresford by Mr. Amherst, the gentleman who made the Kent matches. In those days, except around our parts, Farnham and the Surrey side of Hampshire, a little play went a long way. Why, no man used to be more talked of than Yalden, and when he came among us we soon made up our minds what the rest of them must be. If you want to know, sir, the time the Hambledon Club was formed, I can tell by this;—when we beat them, in 1780, I heard Mr. Paulett say, 'Here have I been thirty years raising our club, and are we to be beaten by a mere parish?' so there must have been a cricket club that played every week regularly, as long ago as 1750. We used to go as eagerly to a match as if it were two armies fighting; we stood at nothing if we were allowed the time; from our parish to Hambledon is twenty-seven miles, and we used to ride both ways the same day, early and late. At last I and John Wells were about building a cart, you have heard of tax carts, sir; well the tax was put on then, and that stopped us. The members of the Hambledon Club had a caravan to take their eleven about, and used once to play always in velvet caps. Lord Winchelsea's eleven used to play in silver laced hats, and always the dress was knee breeches and stockings. We never thought of knocks; and remember I played against Browne of Brighton too. Certainly you would see a bump heave under the stocking, and even the blood came through; but I never knew a man killed, now you ask the question, and never saw any accident of much consequence, though many an *all but*, in all my experience. Fancy the old fashion before cricket shoes, when I saw John Wells tear a finger nail off against his shoe-buckle in picking up a ball."

" Your book, sir, says much about old Nyren. This Nyren was fifty years old when I began to play; he was our general in the Hambledon matches, but not half a player as we reckon now. He had a small farm and inn near Hambledon, and took care of the ground."

" I remember when many things first came into the game which are common now. The law for leg before wicket was not made, nor much wanted, till Ring, one of our best hitters, was shabby enough to get his leg in the way, and take advantage of the bowlers, and when Tom Taylor, another of the best hitters, did the same, the bowlers found themselves beaten, and the law was passed to make leg before wicket out. The law against jerking was owing to the frightful pace Tom Walker put on, and I believe that Harry also tried something more like the modern throwing bowling, and caused the words against throwing also. Wills was not the inventor of that kind of round bowling; he only revived what was forgotten or new to the young folk.

"The umpires did not formerly pitch the wickets. David Harris used to think a great deal of pitching himself a good-wicket, and took much pains in suiting himself every match day."

"Lord Stowell was fond of cricket. He employed me to make a ground for him at Holt Pound."

In the last century, when the waggon and the packhorse supplied the place of the penny train, there was little opportunity for these frequent meetings of men from distant counties that now puzzles us to remember who is North and who is South, who is Surrey or who is Kent. The matches then were truly county matches, and had more of the spirit of hostile tribes and rival clans. "There was no mistaking the Kent boys," said Beldham, "when they came staring in to the Green Man. A few of us had grown used to London, but Kent and Hampshire men had but to speak, or even show themselves, and you need not ask them which side they were on." So the match seemed like Sir Horace Mann and Lord Winchelsea and their respective tenantry—for when will the feudal system be quite extinct? And there was no little pride and honor in the parishes that sent them up, and many a flagon of ale depending in the farms or the hop grounds they severally represented, as to whether they should, as the spirit-stirring saying was, "prove themselves the better men." "I remember in one match," said Beldham, "in Kent, Ring was playing against David Harris. The game was much against him. Sir Horace Mann was cutting about with his stick among the daisies, and cheering every run,—you would have thought his whole fortune (and he did always bet some hundreds) was staked upon the game; and as a new man was going in, he went across to Ring, and said, 'Ring, carry your bat through and make up all the runs, and I'll give you 10*l.* a-year for life.' Well, Ring was out for sixty runs, and only three to tie, and four to beat, and the last man made them. It was Sir Horace who took Aylward away with him out of Hampshire, but the best bat made but a poor bailiff we heard.

"Cricket was played in Sussex very early, before my day at least; but that there was no good play I know by this, that Richard Newland, of Slinden, in Sussex, as you say, sir, taught old Richard Nyren, and that no Sussex man could be found to play him. Now a second rate player of our parish beat Newland easily; so you may judge what the rest of Sussex then were. But before 1780 there were some good players about

Hambledon and the Surrey side of Hampshire. Crawte, the best of the Kent men, was taken away from us; so you will not be wrong, sir, in writing down that Farnham, and thirty miles round, reared all the best players up to my day, about 1780.

"There were some who were then called 'the old players,' and here Fennex's account quite agreed with Beldham's, including Frame and old Small, who Bennett believed by tradition to have been the man who 'found out cricket,' or brought play to any degree of perfection; also Sueter, the wicket-keeper, who, in those days, had very little stumping to do, and Minshull and Colshorn, all mentioned in Nyren." "These men played puddling about their crease with no freedom. I like to see players upright and well forward, to face the ball like a man. The Duke of Dorset made a match at Dartford Brent between 'the Old Players and the New.'—You laugh, sir," said this tottering silver-haired old man, "but we all were new once;—well I played with the Walkers, John Wells, and the rest of our men, and beat the old ones very easily."

"Tom Walker was the most tedious fellow to bowl to, and the slowest runner between wickets I ever saw. I have seen, in running a four, Noah Mann, as fast as Tom was slow, overtake him, pat him on the back, and say, 'Good name for you is *Walker*, for you never were a runner.' It used to be said that David Harris had once bowled him 170 balls for one run! David was a potter by trade, and in a kind of skittle alley made between hurdles, he used to practise bowling four different balls from one end, and then picking them up he would bowl them back again. His bowling cost him a great deal of practice; but it proved well worth his while, for no man ever bowled like him, and he was always first chosen of all the men in England. *Nil sine labore*, remember young cricketers all. 'Lambert' (not the great player of that name), said Nyren, 'had a most deceitful and teasing way of delivering the ball; he tumbled out the Kent and Surrey men, one after another, as if picked off by a rifle corps. His perfection is accounted for by the circumstance that, when he was tending his father's sheep, he would set up a hurdle or two, and bowl away for hours together.'

"There was some good hitting in those days, though too little defence. Tom Taylor would cut away in fine style, almost after the manner of Mr. Budd. Old Small was among the first members of the Hambledon Club. He began to play about 1750, and Lumpy Stevens at the same time. I can give you some notion of what cricket was in those days, for Lumpy, a very bad bat, as he was well aware, once said to me, 'Beldham, what do you think cricket must have been in those days when I was thought a good batsman?' But fielding was very good as far back as I can remember." Now what Beldham called good fielding must have been good enough. He was himself one of the safest hands at a catch. Mr.

Budd, when past forty, was still one of the quickest men I ever played with, taking always middle wicket, and often, by swift running, doing part of long field's work. Sparks, Fennex, Bennett, and young Small, and Mr. Parry, were first rate, not to mention Deagley, whose style of long stopping in the North and South Match of 1836, made Lord Frederick and Mr. Ward justly proud of so good a representative of the game in their younger days. Albeit, an old player of seventy, describing the merits of all these men, said, " put Mr. King at point, Mr. C. Ridding long-stop, and Mr. Pickering cover, and 1 never saw the man that could beat either of them."

" John Wells was a most dangerous man in a single wicket match, being so dead a shot at a wicket. In a celebrated match Lord Frederick warned the Honorable H. Tuffton to beware of him; but John Wells found an opportunity of maintaining his character by shying down from the side little more than the single stump. Tom Sheridan joined some of our matches, but he was no good but to make people laugh. In our days there were no padded gloves. I have seen Tom Walker rub his bleeding fingers in the dust! David used to say he liked to *rind* him."

" The matches against twenty-two were not uncommon in the last century. In 1788 the Hambledon Club played two-and-twenty at Cold Ash Hill. 'Drawing' between leg and wicket is not a new invention.

Old Small, of 1750, was famous for drawing, and for the greater facility he changed the crooked bat of his day for a straight bat. There was some fine cutting before Saunders' day. Harry Walker was the first, I believe, who brought it to perfection. The next genuine cutter, for they were very scarce (I never called mine cutting, not like that of Saunders at least), was Robinson. Walker and Robinson would wait for the ball all but past the wicket, and cut with great force. Others made good off hits, but did not hit late enough for a good Cut. I would never cut with slow bowling. I believe that Walker, Fennex and myself, first opened the old players' eyes to what could be done with the bat; Walker by cutting, and Fennex and I by forward play: but all improvement was owing to David Harris's bowling. His bowling rose almost perpendicular: it was once pronounced a jerk; it was altogether most extraordinary. For thirteen years I averaged forty-three a match, though frequently I had only one innings; but I never could half play unless runs were really wanted."

## CHAP. IV.

**CRICKET GENERALLY ESTABLISHED AS A NATIONAL GAME BY THE END OF THE LAST CENTURY.**

LITTLE is recorded of the Hambledon Club after the year 1786. It broke up when Old Nyren left it, in 1791. Though in this last year the true old Hambledon Eleven all but beat twenty-two of Middlesex at Lord's. Their cricket-ground on Broadhalfpenny Down, in Hampshire, was so far removed from the many noblemen and gentlemen who had seen and admired the severe bowling of David Harris, the brilliant hitting of Beldham, and the interminable defence of the Walkers, that these worthies soon found a more genial sphere for their energies on the grounds of Kent, Surrey, and Middlesex. Still, though the land was deserted, the men survived, and imparted a knowledge of their craft to gentles and simples far and wide.

Most gladly would we chronicle that these good men and true were actuated by a great and a patriotic spirit, to diffuse an aid to civilization—for such our game claims to be—among their wonder-stricken fellow-countrymen; but, in truth, we confess that "reaping golden opinions" and coins, "from all kinds of men," as well as that indescribable tumult and joyous emotions which attend the ball vigorously propelled or heroically stopped, while hundreds of voices shout applause, that such stirring motives, more powerful far with vain glorious man than any foreshortened view of abstract virtue, tended to the migration of the pride of Hambledon. Still, doubtful though the motive, certain is the fact, that the Hambledon players did carry their bats and stumps out of Hampshire into the adjoining counties, and gradually, like all great commanders, taught their adversaries to conquer too. In some instances, as with Lord Winchelsea, Mr. Amherst, and others, noblemen combined the *utile dulci,* pleasure and business, and retained a great player as a keeper or a bailiff, as Martingell once was engaged by Earl Ducie. In other instances, the play of the summer led to employment through the winter; or else these busy bees lived on the sweets of their sunshine toil, enjoying *otium cum dignitate*—that is, living like gentlemen, with nothing to do.

This accounts for our finding these Hampshire men playing Kent matches; being, like a learned Lord in Punch's picture, "naturalized everywhere," or citizens of the world.

Let us trace these Hambledonians in all their contests, from the date mentioned (1786 to 1800), the eventful period of the French Revolution and Nelson's victories, and see how the Bank stopping payment, the mutiny of the fleet, and the threatened invasion, put together, did not prevent balls from flying over the tented field, in a far more innocent and rational way on this than on the other side of the water.

Now, what were the matches in the last century—"eleven gentlemen against the twelve Cæsars?" No! these, though ancient names, are of modern times. Kent and England was as good an annual match in the last as in the present century. The White Conduit Fields and the Artillery Ground supplied the place of Lord's, though in 1787 the name of Lord's is found in Bentley's Matches, implying, of course, the old Marylebone Ground, now Dorset Square, under Thomas Lord, and not the present by St. John's Wood, more properly deserving the name of Dark's than Lord's. The Kentish battle-fields were Sevenoaks, the land of Clout, one of the original makers of cricket-balls; Coxheath, Dandelion Fields, in the Isle of Thanet, and Cobham Park; also Dartford Brent and Pennenden Heath; there is also early mention of Gravesend, Rochester, and Woolwich.

Next in importance to the Kent matches were those of Hampshire and of Surrey, with each of which counties indifferently the Hambledon men used to play. For it must not be supposed that the whole county of Surrey put forth a crop of stumps and wickets all at once: we have already said that malt and hops and cricket have ever gone together. Two parishes in Surrey, adjoining Hants, won the original laurels for their county, and those in the immediate vicinity of the Farnham hop county. The Holt, near Farnham, and Moulsey Hurst, were the Surrey grounds. The match might truly have been called " Farnham's hop-gatherers *v.* those of Kent." The former, aided occasionally by men who drank the ale of Alton, just as Burton-on-Trent, life-sustainer to our Indian empire, sends forth its giants, refreshed with bitter ale, to defend the honor of the neighboring towns and counties. The men of Hampshire, after Broadhalfpenny was abandoned to docks and thistles, pitched their tents generally either upon Windmill Downs or upon Stoke Downs; and once they played a match against T. Asheton Smith, whose mantle has descended on a worthy representative, whether on the level turf or by the cover's side. Albeit, when that gentleman has a "meet," as occasionally advertised at Hambledon, he must unconsciously avoid the spot where " titch and turn"—the Hampshire cry—did once exhilarate the famous James Aylward, among others, as he astonished the Farnham waggoner, by continuing one and the same innings as the man drove up on the Tuesday afternoon and down on the Wednesday morning. This match was played at Andover, and the surnames of most of the Eleven may be read on the tombstones, with the best of characters, in Andover Churchyard. Bourne Paddock, Earl Darnley's estate, and Burley Park, in Rutlandshire, constituted often the debatable ground in their respective counties. Earl Darnley, as well as Sir Horace Mann and Earl Winchelsea, Mr. Paulett and Mr. East, lent their names and patronage to Elevens; sometimes in the places mentioned, sometimes at Lord's, and sometimes at Perriam Downs, near Luggershal, in Wiltshire.

Middlesex also, exclusively of the Marylebone Club, had its Eleven in these days; or, we should say, its *twenty-two*, for that was the number then required to stand the disciplined forces of Hampshire, Kent, or England. And this reminds us of an "Uxbridge ground," where Middlesex played and lost, and "Hornchurch, Essex," where Essex, in 1791, was sufficiently advanced to win against Marylebone, an occasion memorable, because Lord Frederic Beauclerk there played his first recorded match, making scarce any runs, but bowling four wickets. "There was also," writes the Hon. R. Grimstone, "'the Bowling-green,' at Harrow-on-the-Hill, where the school played: Richardson, who subsequently became Mr. Justice Richardson, was the captain of the School Eleven in 1782."

Already, in 1790, the game was spreading northwards, or, rather, proofs exist that it had long before struck far and wide its roots and branches in northern latitudes; and also that it was a game as popular with the men of labor as the men of leisure, and therefore incontestably of home growth: no mere exotic, or importation, of the favored few can cricket be, if, like its namesake, it is found "a household word" with those whom Burns aptly calls "the many-aproned sons of mechanical life."

In 1791, Eton, that is, the old Etonians, played Marylebone, four players given on either side; and all true Etonians will thank us for informing them, not only that the seven Etonians were more than a match for their adversaries, but also that this match proves that Eton had, at that early date, the honor of sending forth the most distinguished amateurs of the day; for Lord Winchelsea, Hon. H. Fitzroy, Earl Darnley, Hon. E. C. Bligh, C. Anguish, Asheton Smith — good men and true—were Etonians all. This match was played in Burley Park, Rutlandshire, on the following day, June 25th, 1791: the Marylebone played eleven yeomen and artisans of Leicester; and though the Leicestrians cut a sorry figure, still the fact that the Midland Counties practised cricket sixty years ago is worth recording. Peter Heward, of Leicester, a famous wicket-keeper, of twenty years since, told me of a trial match in which he saw his father, quite an old man, with another veteran of his own standing, quickly put out with the old-fashioned slow bowling for some twenty runs a really good Eleven—good, that is, against the modern style of bowling; and cricket was not a new game in this old man's early days (say 1780) about Leicester and Nottingham, as the score in page 33, alone would prove; for such a game as cricket, evidently of gradual development, must have been played in some primitive form many a long year before the date of 1775, in which it had excited sufficient interest, and was itself sufficiently matured in form to show the two Elevens of Sheffield and of Nottingham. Add to this, what we have already mentioned, a rude form of cricket as far north as Angus and Lothian in 1700, and we can hardly doubt that cricket was known as early in the Midland as in the Southern Counties. The men of Nottingham—land of Clarke, Barker, and of Redgate—next month, in the same year (1791), threw down the gauntlet, and shared the same fate; and next day the Marylebone, " adding," in a cricketing sense, " insult unto injury," played twenty-two of them, and won by thirteen runs.

In 1790, the shopocracy of Brighton had also an Eleven; and Sussex and Surrey, in 1792, sent an eleven against England to Lord's, who scored the longest number in one innings on record—453 runs! " M. C. C. v. twenty-two of Nottingham," we now find an annual match; and also " M. C. C. v. Brighton," which becomes at once worthy of the fame that Sussex long has borne. In 1793, the old Westminster men all but beat the old Etonians: and Essex and Herts, too near not to emulate the fame of Kent and Surrey, were content, like second-rate performers, to have, though playing twenty-two, one benefit between them, in the shape of defeat in one innings from England. And here we are reminded by two old players, a Kent and an Essex man, that, being schoolboys in 1785, they can respectively testify that, both in Kent and in Essex, cricket appeared to them more of a village game than they have ever seen it of late years. "There was a cricket-bat behind the door, or else up in the bacon rack, in every cottage. We heard little of clubs, except around London; still the game was played by many or by few, in every school and village green in Essex and in Kent, and the field placed much as when with the Sidmouth I played the Teignbridge Club in 1826. Mr. Whitehead was the great hitter of Kent; and Frame and Small were names as often mentioned as Pilch and Parr by our boys now." And now (1793) the game had penetrated further West; for eleven yeomen at Oldfield Bray, in Berkshire, had learned long enough to defeat a good eleven of the Marylebone Club.

In 1795, the Hon. Colonel Lennox, memorable for a duel with the Duke of York, fought on the cricket ground at Dartford Brent, headed Elevens against the Earl of Winchelsea; and now, first the Marylebone eleven beat sixteen Oxonians on Bullingdon Green.

In 1797, the Montpelier Club and ground attract our notice. The name of this club is one of the most ancient, and their ground a short distance only from the ground of Hall of Camberwell.

Swaffham, in Norfolk, is now mentioned for the first time. But Norfolk lies out of the usual road, and is a county that, as Mr. Dickens said of Golden Square, before it was the residence of Cardinal Wiseman, "is nobody's way to or from any place." So, in those slow coach and pack-horse days, the patrons of Kent, Surrey, Hants, and Marylebone, who alone gave to what else were " airy nothing, a local habitation and a name," could not so easily extend their circuit to the land of turkeys, lithotomy, and dumplings. But it happened once that Lord Frederic Beauclerk was heard to say, his eleven should beat any three elevens in the county of Norfolk; whence arose a challenge from the Norfolk men, whom, sure enough, his Lordship did beat, and that in one innings; and a print, though not on pocket-handkerchiefs, was struck off to perpetuate this honorable achievement.

Lord F. Beauclerk was now one of the first batsmen of his day; as also were the Hon. H. and I. Tuffton; and frequently headed a division of the Marylebone, or some county club, against Middlesex, and even Hampstead and Highgate.

In this year (1798) these gentlemen aforesaid made the first attempt at a Gentlemen and Players' match; and on this first occasion the players won; but when we mention that they had three players given, and also that T. Walker, Beldham, and Hammond were the three, certainly it was like playing England, "the part of England being left out by particular desire."

Kent attacked England in 1798, but, being beaten in about *half* an innings, we find the Kentish men, in 1800, though still hankering after that cosmopolitan distinction, modestly accept the odds of nineteen, and afterwards play twenty-three men to twelve.

The chief patronage, and consequently the chief practice, in cricket, was beyond all comparison in London. There the play was nearly all professional: even the gentlemen made a profession of it; and, therefore, though cricket was far more extensively spread throughout the villages of Kent than of Middlesex, the clubs of the metropolis figure in the score books as defying all competition. Professional players, we may observe, have always a decided advantage in respect of judicious choice and mustering their best men. The best eleven players are almost always known, and can be mustered on a given day. Neither favor, friendship, nor etiquette interferes with their election; but the eleven gentlemen of England can never be anything more than the best eleven known to the party who make the match, and such as can spare the time and money which the match demands.

Having now traced the rise and progress of the game to the time of its general establishment till the time that Beldham had shown the full powers of the bat and Lord Frederic had, as Fennex always declared, formed his style upon Beldham's; and since now we approach the era of a new school, and the forward play of Fennex,—which his father termed an innovation and presumption " contrary to all experience,"—till the same forward play was proved effectual by Lambert; and Hammond had shown that, in spite of wicket keepers, bowling, if slow especially, might be met and hit away at the pitch; now we will wait to characterize, in the words of eye-witnesses, the heroes of the contests already mentioned.

Of the old players I may be brief, because the few old gentlemen (with one of whom I am in daily communication) who have heard even the names of the Walkers, Frame, Small, and David Harris, are passing away, full of years, and almost all their written history consists in undiscriminating scores.

In point of style, the old players did not play the steady game with maiden overs as at present. The defensive was comparatively unknown: both the bat and the wicket, and the style of bowling too, were all adapted to a short life and a merry one. The wooden substitute for a ball, as in Cat and Dog, before described, evidently implied a hitting, and not a stopping game.

The wicket, as we collect from a MS. furnished by an old friend to the late William Ward, Esq., was, in the early days of the Hambledon Club, one foot high and two feet wide, consisting of two stumps only, with one stump laid across. Thus straight balls passed between, and what we now call well pitched balls would of course rise over. Where, then, was the encouragement to block, when fortune would so often serve the place of science? And, as to the bat, look at the picture of cricket as played in the old Artillery Ground; the bat is curved at the end like a hockey stick, or the handle of a spoon,—and as common implements usually are adapted to the work to be performed, you will readily believe that in olden time the freest hitter was the best batsman. The bowling was all along the ground, hand and eye being everything, and judgment nothing, because the art originally was to bowl under the bat; the wicket was too low for rising balls; and the reason we hear sometimes of the block hole was, not that the block hole originally denoted guard, but because between these two-feet-asunder stumps there was cut a hole big enough to contain the ball, and, as now with the scool boy's game of rounders, the hitter was made out in running a notch by the ball being popped into this hole (whence popping crease) before the point of the bat could reach it.

Did we say running a notch? *unde* notch? What wonder ere the days of useful knowledge, and Sir William Curtis's three R's, or reading, writing, and arithmetic, that natural science should be evolved in a truly natural way; what wonder that notches on a stick like the notches in the milk-woman's tally in Hogarth's picture, should supply the place of those complicated papers of vertical columns, which subject the bowling, the batting, and the fielding to a process severely and scrupulously just, of analytical observation, or differential calculus. Where now there sit on kitchen chairs, with ink bottle tied to a stump the worse for wear, Messrs. Caldecourt and Bailey ('tis pity two such men should ever not be umpires), with an uncomfortable length of paper on their knees, and large tin telegraphic letters above their heads; and where now is Lillywhite's printing press to hand down every hit as soon as made on twopenny cards to the next generation; there, or in a similar position, old Frame, or young Small (young once: he died in 1834, aged eighty) might have placed a trusty yeoman to cut notches with his bread and bacon knife on an ashen stick. Oh! 'tis enough to make the Hambledon heroes sit upright in their graves with astonishment to think that, in the Gentlemen and Players' Match, in 1850, the cricketers of old Sparkes' Ground, at Edinburgh, could actually know the score of the first innings in London, almost as soon as the second had commenced.

But when we say that the old players had little or nothing of the defensive, we speak of the play before 1780, when David Harris flourished: for William Beldham distinctly assured us that the art of bowling over the bat by " length balls " originated with the famous David. An assertion, we will venture to say, which requires a little, and only a little qualification. Length bowling, or three quarter balls, to use a popular, though exploded, expression, was introduced in David's time, and by him first brought to perfection. And what rather confirms this statement is, that the early bowlers, were very swift bowlers,—such was not only David, but the famous Brett, of earlier date, and Frame of great renown: a more moderate pace resulted from the new discovery of a well pitched bail ball.

The old players well understood the art of twisting, or bias bowling. Lambert, "the little farmer," says Nyren, "improved on the art, and puzzled the Kent men in a great match, by twisting the reverse of the usual way,—that is, from the off to the leg stump." Tom Walker tried what Nyren calls the throwing-bowling, and defied all the players of the day to withstand this novelty; but, by a council of the Hambledon Club, this was forbidden, and Wills, a Sussex man, had the praise of inventing it some twenty years later. In a notable match of the Hambledon Club, it was observed, at a critical point of the game, that the ball passed three times between the two stumps without knocking off the bail; and then, first about 1780, a third stump was added, and, seeing that the new style of balls which rise over the bat rose also over the wickets, then but one foot high, the wicket was altered to the dimensions of 22 inches by 6, at which measure it remained till about 1814, when it was increased to 26 inches by 8, and again to its present dimensions of 27 inches by 8 in 1817.

David Harris' bowling, Fennex used to say, introduced, or at least established and fixed, a steady and defensive style of batting. " I have seen," said Sparks, " seventy or eighty runs in an innings, though not more than eight or nine made at Harris's end." " Harris," said an excellent judge, who well remembers him, " attained nearly all the quickness of rise and height of delivery, of the over-hand bowling, with far greater straightness and precision. The ball appeared to be forced out from under his arm with some unaccountable jerk, so that it was delivered breast-high. His precision exceeded anything I have ever seen, insomuch that Tom Walker declared that, on one occasion, where turf was thin, and the color of the soil readily appeared, one spot was positively uncovered by the repeated pitching of David's balls in the same place." " This bowling," said Sparkes, " compelled you to make the best of your reach forward ; for if you let the ball pitch too near and crowd upon you, no player could possibly prevent a mistake from the height and' rapidity with which it cut up the ground." This account agrees with the well-known description of Nyren. " Harris's mode of delivering the ball was very singular. He would bring it from under the arm by a twist, and nearly as high as his arm-pit, and with this action push it, as it were, from him. How it was that the balls acquired the velocity they did by this mode of delivery, I never could comprehend. His balls were very little beholden to the ground; it was but a touch and up again; and woe be to the man who did not get in to block then, for they had such a peculiar curl they would grind his fingers against the bat."

And Nyren agrees with my informants in ascribing great improvement in batting, and he specifies, " particularly in stopping " (for the act of defence, we said, was not essential to the batsman in the ideas of one of the old players), to the bowling of David Harris, and bears testimony to an assertion, that forward play, that is, meeting at the pitch balls considerably short of a half volley, was little known to the oldest players, and was called into requisition chiefly by the bowling of David Harris. Obviously, with the primitive fashion of ground bowling, called sneakers, forward play could have no place, and even well-pitched balls, like those of Noah Mann, *alias* Lumpy, of moderate pace might be played with some effect, even behind the crease; but David Harris, with pace, pitch, and rapid rise combined, imperatively demanded a new invention, and such was forward play about 1800. Old Fennix, who died, alas! in a Middlesex workhouse, aged eighty, in 1839 (had his conduct been as straightforward and upright as his bat, he would have known a better end), always declared that he was the first, and remained long without followers; and no small praise is due to the boldness and originality that set at nought the received maxims of his forefathers before he was born or thought of; daring to try things that, had they been ordinarily reasonable, would not, of course, have been ignored by Frame, by Pinchase, nor by Small. The world wants such men as Fennex; men, who, like the late lamented Sir Robert Peel, will shake off the prejudices of birth, parentage, and education, and boldly declare that age has taught them wisdom, and that the policy of their predecessors, however expensively stereotyped, must be revised and corrected and adapted to the demands of a more inquiring generation. "My father," said Fennex, "asked me how I came by that new play, reaching out as no one ever saw before." The same style he lived to see practised, not elegantly, but with wonderful power and effect by Lambert, "a most severe and resolute hitter;" and Fennix also boasted that he had a most proficient disciple in Fuller Pilch: though I suspect—that as "*poeta nascitur non fit;*" that is, that all great performers appear to have brought the secret of their excellence into the world along with them, and are not the mere puppets of which others pull the strings—that Fuller Pilch may think he rather coincided with than learnt from William Fennex.

Now the David Harris aforesaid, who wrought quite a revolution in the game, changing cricket from a backward and a slashing to a forward and defensive game, and claiming higher stumps to do justice to his skill—this David, whose bowling was many years before his generation, having all the excellence of Lillywhite's high delivery, though free from all imputation of unfairness—this David rose early, and late took rest, and ate the bread of carefulness, before he attained such distinction as, in these days of railroads, Thames tunnels, and tubular gloves and bridges, to deserve the notice of our pen. " For," said John Bennett, " you might have seen David practising at dinner time and after hours, all the winter through;" and "many a Hampshire barn," said Beagley, " has been heard to resound with bats and balls as well as threshing." And now we must mention the men, who, at the end of the last century, represented the Pilch, the Parr, the Wenman, and the Wisden of the present day.

Lord Beauclerk was formed on the style of Beldham, whom, in brilliancy of hitting, he nearly resembled. The Hon. H. Bligh and Hon. H. Tufton were of the same school. Sir Peter Burrell was also a good hitter, and these were the most distinguished gentlemen players of the day. Earl Winchelsea was in every principal match, but rather for his patronage than his play: and the Hon. Col. Lennox for the same reason. Mr. R. Whitehead was a Kent player of great celebrity. But Lord F. Beauclerk was the only gentleman who had any claim in the last century to play in an All England eleven. He was also one of the fastest runners.

Hammond was the great wicket-keeper; but then the bowling was slow: Sparkes said he saw him catch out Robinson by a draw between leg and wicket. Freemantle was the first long stop; but Ray the finest field in England; and in those days, when the scores were long, fielding was of even more consideration than at present. Of the professional players, Beldham, Hammond, Tom and Harry Walker, Freemantle, Robinson, Fennex, J. Wells, and J. Small were the first chosen after Harris had passed away; for Nyren says that even Lord Beauclerk could hardly have seen David Harris in his prime. At this time there was a sufficient number of players to maintain the credit of the left hands. On the 10th of May, 1790, the Left-handed beat the Right by thirty-nine runs. This match reveals that Harris and Aylward, and the three best Kent players, Brazier, Crawte, and Clifford, — Sueter, the first distinguished wicket-keeper, — H. Walker, and Freemantle were all left-handed: so also was Noah Mann.

The above mentioned players are quite sufficient to give some idea of the play of the last century. Sparkes is well known to the author of these pages as his quondam instructor. In batting, he differed not widely from the usual style of good players, save that he never played forward to any very great extent. Playing under leg, according to the old fashion (we call it old-fashion though Pilch adopts it,) served instead of the far more elegant and efficient "draw." Sparkes was also a fair bias bowler, but of no great pace, and not very difficult. I remember his saying that the old school of slow bowling was beaten by Hammond setting the example of running in. "Hammond," he said, " on one occasion, hit back a slow ball to Lord F. Beauclerk with such frightful force that it just skimmed his Lordship's unguarded head, and he had scarcely nerve to bowl after. Of Fennex, we can also speak from our friend Rev. John Mitford. Fennex was a fair straight-forward hitter, and once as good a single wicket-player as any in England. His attitude was easy, and he played elegantly, and hit well from the wrist. If his bowling was any specimen of that of his contemporaries, they were by no means to be despised. His bowling was very swift and of high delivery, the ball cut and ground up with great quickness and precision. Fennex used to say that the men of the present day had little idea of what the old underhand bowling really could effect; and, from the specimen which Fennex himself gave at sixty-five years of age, there appeared to be much reason in his assertion. Of all the players Fennex had ever seen (for some partiality for by-gone days we must of course allow) none elicited his notes of admiration like Beldham. We cannot compare a man who played underhand with those who are formed on overhand bowling. Still there is reason to believe what Mr. Ward and others have told us, that

Beldham had that genius for cricket, that wonderful eye (although it failed him very early), and quickness of hand, that would have made him a great player in any age.

Beldham related to us, in 1838, and that with no little nimbleness of hand and vivacity of eye, while he suited the action to the word with a bat of his own manufacture, how he had drawn forth the plaudits of Lords as he hit round and helped on the bowling of Browne, of Brighton, even faster than before, though the good men of Brighton thought that no one could stand against him, and Browne had thought to bowl Beldham off his legs. This match of Hants against England in 1819 Fennex was fond of describing, and certainly it gives some idea of what Beldham could do. "Osbaldeston," said Mr. Ward, "with his tremendously fast bowling, was defying every one at single wicket, and he and Lambert challenged Mr. E. H. Budd with three others. Just then I had seen Browne's swift bowling, and a hint from me settled the match. Browne was engaged, and Osbaldeston was beaten with his own weapons." A match was now made to give Browne a fair trial, and "we were having a social glass," said Fennex, "and talking over with Beldham the match of the morrow at the 'Green Man,' when Browne came in, and told Beldham, with as much sincerity as good-humor, that he should soon send his stumps a-flying." "Hold there," said Beldham, fingering his bat, "you will be good enough to allow me this bit of wood, won't you?" "Certainly," said Browne. "Quite satisfied," answered Beldham, "so to-morrow you shall see." "Seventy-two runs," said Fennex, and the score book attests his accuracy, "was Beldham's first and only innings," and Beagley also joined with Fennex, and assured us, that he never saw a more complete triumph of a batsman over a bowler. Nearly every ball was cut or slipped away till Browne hardly dared to bowl within his reach.

We desire not to qualify the praises of Beldham, but when we hear that he was unrivalled in elegant and brilliant hitting, and in that wonderful versatility that cut indifferently, quick as lightning, all round him, we cannot help remarking, that such bowling as that of Redgate or Wisden renders imperatively necessary a severe style of defence, and an attitude of cautious watchfulness, that must render the batsman not quite such a picture for the artist as might be seen in the days of Beldham and Lord F. Beauclerk.

So far we have traced the diffusion of the game and the degrees of proficiency attained to the beginning of the present century. To sum up the evidence, by the year 1800, cricket had become the pastime even of the common people in Hampshire, Surrey, Sussex, and Kent; and had been introduced into the adjoining counties, and though we cannot trace its continuity beyond Rutlandshire and Burley Park, certainly it had been long familiar to the men of Leicester and of Nottingham and Sheffield. That, in point of skill, Fielding, generally, was already as good, and quite as much valued in a match as it has been since; and Wicket-keeping in particular had been ably executed by Sueter, for he could stump off Brett, whose pace Nyren, acquainted as he was with all the bowlers to the days of Lillywhite, called quite of the steam-engine power, albeit no wicket-keeper could shine like Wenman or Box, except with the regularity of overhand bowling; and already Bowlers had attained by bias and quick delivery all the excellence which underhand bowling admits. Still, as regards Batting, the very fact that the stumps remained six inches wide, by twenty-two inches in height, undeniably proves that the secret of success was limited to comparatively a small number of players.

## CHAP. V.

##### THE FIRST TWENTY YEARS OF THE PRESENT CENTURY.

BEFORE this century was one year old, David Harris, Harry Walker, Purchase, Aylward, and Lumpy had left the stage, and John Small, instead of hitting bad balls whose stitches would not last a match, had learnt to make commodities so good that Clout's and Duke's were mere toyshop in comparison. Noah Mann was the Caldecourt, or umpire, of the day, and Harry Bentley also, when he did not play. Five years more saw nearly the last of Earl Winchelsea, Sir Horace Mann, Earl Darnley, and Lord Yarmouth; still Surrey had a generous friend in Mr. Laurell, Hants in Mr. T. Smith, and Kent in the Honorables H. and J. Tuffton. The Pavilion at Lord's, then and since 1787 on the site of Dorset Square, was attended by Lord Frederick Beauclerk, then a young man of four-and-twenty, the Honorables Colonel Bligh, General Lennox, H. and J. Tuffton, and A. Upton. Also, there were usually Messrs. R. Whitehead, G. Leycester, S. Vigne, and F. Ladbroke. These were the great promoters of the matches, and the first of the amateurs. Cricket, we have shown, was originally classed among the games of the lower orders; so we find the yeomen infinitely superior to the gentlemen even before cricket had become by any means so much of a profession as it is now. Tom Walker, Beldham, John Wells, Fennex, Hammond, Robinson, Lambert, Sparkes, H. Bentley, Bennett, Freemantle, were the best professionals of the day. For it was seven or eight years later that E. H. Budd, and his unequal rival, Mr. Brand, and his sporting friend, Osbaldeston, as also that fine player, E. Parry, Esq., severally appeared; and later still, that Mr. Ward, Howard, Beagley, Thumwood, Caldecourt, Slater, Flavel, Ashby, Searle, and Saunders, successively showed every resource of bias bowling to shorten the scores, and of fine hitting to lengthen them. By the end of these twenty years, all these distinguished players had taught a game in which the batting beat the bowling. Matches took up three days; the wicket had been twice enlarged, once about 1814, and again about 1817; old Lord had tried his third, the present, ground; the Legs had taught the wisdom of playing rather for love than money; slow coaches had given way to fast, long whist to short, and ultimately Lambert, John Wells, Howard, and Powell, handed over the ball to Broadbridge and Lillywhite.

Such is the scene, the characters, and the performance. Matches in those days were more numerously attended than now, said Mr. Ward: he thought that the old game was more attractive, because more busy, than the new. Tom Lord's flag was the well known telegraph that brought him in from three to four thousand sixpences at a match. John Goldham, the octogenarian inspector of Billingsgate, has seen the Duke of York and his adversary, Honorable Colonel Lennox, in the same game, and had the honor of playing with both, and the Prince Regent, too, in the White Conduit Fields, on which spot Mr. Goldham built his present house. Great matches, in those days, as in these, cost money. Six guineas to win and four to lose was the player's fee, or five and three if they lived in town. So as every match cost some seventy pounds, over the fire-place at Lord's you would see a Subscription List for Surrey against England, or for England against Kent, as the case might be, and find notices at Brookes's and other clubs.

But what were the famed cricket Counties in these twenty years? The glory of Kent had for a time departed. Time was when Kent could challenge England man for man, but now only with such odds as twenty-three to twelve. As to its wide extension, cricket advanced but slowly compared with recent times. Still a small circle round London would comprise all the finest players. It was not till 1820 that Norfolk, forgetting its three Elevens beaten by Lord Frederick, again played Marylebone, and though three gentlemen were given and Fuller Pilch played—then a lad of seventeen years—Norfolk lost by 417 runs, including Mr. Ward's longest score on record,—278. " But he was missed," said Mr. Budd, " the easiest possible catch before he had scored thirty." Kennington Oval, perhaps, was then all docks and thistles. Still Surrey was the first cricket county, and Mr. Laurell (Robinson was his keeper; an awful man for poachers, 6 feet 1 inch, and 16 stone, and strong in proportion), most generous of supporters, was not slow to give orders on Lord for golden guineas, when a Surrey man by catch, or innings, called forth applause. Of the same high order were Sir J. Cope of Bramshill Park and Mr. Barnett, the banker, promoter of the B. matches; Hon. D. Kinnaird, and Mr. W. Ward, who, by purchase of a lease, saved Lord's from building ground; an act of generosity in which he imitated the good old Duke of Dorset, who, said Mr. Budd, " gave the ground called the Vine, at Sevenoaks, to the use of cricketers for ever."

The good men of Surrey, in 1800, monopolized nearly all the play of England. Lord Frederick Beauclerk and Hammond were the only All England players not Surrey men.

Kent had then some civil contests—petty wars of single clans—but no county match; and their great friend, R. Whitehead, Esq., depended on the M.C.C. for his finest games. The game had become a profession: a science to the gentlemen, and an art or handicraft to the players; and Farnham found in London the best market for its cricket as for its hops. The best Kent play was displayed at Rochester, and yet more at Woolwich, but chiefly among our officers, whose bats were bought in London, not at Sevenoaks. Games reflecting none such honor to the county as when the Earls of Thanet and of Darnley brought their own tenantry to Lord's or Dartford Brent, armed with the native willow wood of Kent. So the Honorables H. and A. Tuffton were obliged to yield to the altered times, and play two-and-twenty men where their noble father, the Earl of Thanet, had won with eleven. "Thirteen to twenty-three was the number we enjoyed," said Sparkes, "for with thirteen good men well-placed, and the bowling good, we did not want their twenty-three. A third man on, and a forward point, or kind of middle wicket, with slow bowling, or an extra slip with fast, made a very strong field: the Kent men were sometimes regularly pounded."

In 1805, we find a curious match: the "twelve best against twenty-three next best." Lord Frederick was the only amateur among the former; but Barton, one of the "next best" among the latter, proved worth 100 runs! Mr. Budd first appeared at Lord's in 1808, and was among the longest scorers from the very first.

The Homerton Club also furnished an annual match:

still all within the sound of Bow bells. "To forget Homerton," said Mr. Ward, "were to ignore Mr. Vigne, our wicket-keeper, but one of very moderate powers. Hammond was the best we ever had. He played till his sixtieth year; but Browne and Osbaldestone put all wicket-keeping to the rout. Hammond's great success was in the days of slow bowling. John Wells and Howard were the two best fast bowlers, though Powell was very true. Osbaldestone beat his side with byes and slips—thirty byes in the B. match." Few men could hit him before wicket; whence the many single wicket-matches he played; but Mr. Ward put an end to his reign by finding out Browne of Brighton. Beagley said of Browne, as the players now say of Mr. Fellows, they had no objection to him when the ground was smooth.

The Homerton Club also boasted of Mr. Ladbroke, one of the great promoters of matches, as well as the late Mr. Aislaby, always fond of the game, but all his life "too big to play,"—the remark by Lord Frederick of Mr. Ward, which, being repeated, did no little to develop the latent powers of that most efficient player.

The Montpelier Club, also, with men given, annually played Marylebone.

Lord Frederick, in 1803, gave a little variety to the matches by leading against Marylebone ten men of Leicester and Nottingham with the two Warsops. "T. Warsop," said Clarke, "was one of the best bowlers I ever knew." Clarke has also a high opinion of Lambert, from whom he learnt more of the game than from any other man.

Lambert's bowling was like Mr. Budd's, against which I have often played : a high underhand delivery, slow, but rising very high, very accurately pitched, and turning in from leg stump. " About the year 1818, Lambert and I," said Mr. Budd, " attained to a kind of round-armed delivery (described as Clarke's), by which we rose decidedly superior to all the batsmen of the day. Mr. Ward could not play it, but he headed a party against us, and our new bowling was ignored." Tom Walker and Lord Frederick were of the tediously slow school; Lambert and Budd several degrees faster. Howard and John Wells were the fast underhand bowlers.

Lord Frederick was a very successful bowler, but was at last beat by men running into him. Sparks mentioned another player, who brought very slow bowling to perfection, and beat in the same way. Beldham thought Mr. Budd's bowling better than Lord Frederick's.

His Lordship is generally supposed to have been the best amateur of his day—an assertion I can by no means reconcile with acknowledged facts; for Mr. Budd made the best average, though usually placed against Lambert's bowling, and playing almost exclusively in the great matches. Mr. Budd was a much more powerful hitter. Lord Frederick said, "Budd always wanted to win the game off a single ball:" Beldham observed, " if Mr. Budd would not hit so eagerly, he would be the finest player in all England." When I knew him, his hitting was quite safe play.

But since Mr. Budd had the largest average in spite of his hitting, Beldham becomes a witness in his favor. Mr. Budd measured five feet ten inches, and weighed twelve stone, very clean made and powerful, with an eye singularly keen, and great natural quickness, being one of the fastest runners of his day. He stood usually at middle wicket. I never saw safer hands at a catch; and I have seen him very quick at stumping out. But Lord Frederick could not take every part of the field; but was always short slip, and not one of the very best. Mr. Budd hit well with the wrist. At Woolwich he hit a volley to long field for *nine*, though Parry threw it in. He also hit out of Lord's old ground. "Lord had said he would forfeit twenty-five guineas if any one thus proved his ground too small; so we all crowded around Budd," said Beldham, " and told him what he might claim. 'Well, then,' he said, 'I claim it, and give it among the players.' But Lord was shabby, and would not pay." Mr. Budd is now in his sixty-sixth year, still I have never seen the country Eleven that could spare him yet.

Lambert was also good at every point. In batting, he was a bold, forward player. He stood with left foot a yard in advance, swaying his bat and body as if to attain momentum, and reaching forward almost to where the ball must pitch.

Lambert's chief point was to take the ball at the pitch and drive it powerfully away, "and," said Mr. Budd, "to a slow bowler his return was so quick and forcible, that his whole manner was really intimidating to a bowler." Every one remarked how completely Lambert seemed master of the ball. Usually the bowler appears to attack, and the batsman to defend; but Lambert seemed always on the attack, and the bowler at his mercy, and "hit," said Beldham, "what no one else could meddle with."

Lord Frederick was formed on Beldham's style. Mr. Budd's position at the wicket was much the same: the right foot placed as usual, but the left rather behind, and nearly a yard apart, so that instead of the upright bat and figure of Pilch, the bat was drawn across, and the figure hung away from the wicket. This was a mistake. Before the ball could be played, Mr. Budd was too good a player not to be up, like Pilch, and play well over his off stump. Still Mr. Budd explained to me that this position of the left foot was just where one naturally shifts it to have room for a cut; so this strange attitude was supposed to favor their fine off hits. I say Off hit, because the Cut did not properly belong to either of these players: Robinson and Saunders were the men to cut,—cutting balls clean away from the bails, though Robinson had a maimed hand, burnt when a child: the handle of his bat was grooved to fit his stunted fingers. Talking of his bat, the players once discovered by measurement it was beyond the statute width, and would not pass through the standard. So, unceremoniously, a knife was produced, and the bat reduced to rather its just than fair proportions. "Well," said Robinson, "I'll pay you off for spoiling my bat;" and sure enough he did, hitting tremendously, and making one of his largest innings, which were often near a hundred runs.

During these twenty years, Hampshire, like Kent, had lost its renown, but simply because Hambledon was now no more; nor did Surrey and Hampshire any longer count as one. To confirm our assertion that Farnham produced the players,—for in 1808, Surrey had played and beat England three times in one season, and from 1820 to 1825 Godalming is mentioned as the most powerful antagonist; but, whether called Godalming or Surrey, we must not forget that the locality is the same—we observe, that, in 1821, M. C. C. plays "The Three Parishes," namely, Godalming, Farnham, and Hartley Row, which parishes, after rearing the finest cotemporaries of Beldham, then boasted a later race of players in Flavel, Searle, Howard, Thumwood, Mathews.

"About this time (July 23, 1821)," said Beldham, " we played the Coronation Match; ' M. C. C. against the Players of England.' We scored 278 and only six wickets down, when the game was given up. I was hurt and could not run my notches; still James Bland, and the other Legs, begged of me to take pains, for it was no sporting match, 'any odds and no takers;' and they wanted to shame the gentlemen against wasting their (the Legs') time in the same way another time."

But the day for Hampshire, as for Kent, was doomed to shine again. Fennex, Small, the Walkers, J. Wells, and Hammond, in time drop off from Surrey,—and about the same time, 1815, Caldecourt, Holloway, Beagley, Thumwood, Shearman, Howard, Mr. Ward, and Mr. Knight, restore the balance of power for Hants, as afterwards, Broadbridge and Lillywhite for Sussex.

"In 1817, we went," said Mr. Budd, "with Osbaldestone to play twenty-two of Nottingham. In that match Clarke played. In common with others I lost my money, and was greatly disappointed at the termination. One paid player was accused of selling, and never employed after. The concourse of people was very great: these were the days of the Luddites (rioters), and the magistrates warned us, that, unless we would stop our game at seven o'clock, they could not answer for keeping the peace. At seven o'clock we stopped, and simultaneously the thousands who lined the ground began to close in upon us. Lord Frederick lost nerve and was very much alarmed; but

I said they didn't want to hurt us. "No; they simply came to have a look at the eleven men who ventured to play two for one." His Lordship broke his finger, and, batting with one hand, scored only eleven runs. Nine men, the largest number perhaps on record, are recorded as "caught by Budd."

Just before the establishment of Mr. Will's round-hand bowling, as if to prepare the way, Ashby came forth with an unusual bias, but no great pace. Sparkes bowled in the same style; as also Matthews and Mr. Jenner somewhat later. Still the batsmen were full as powerful as ever, reckoning Saunders, Searle, Beagley, Messrs. Ward, Kingscote, Knight; Suffolk became very strong with Pilch, the Messrs. Blake, and others, of the famous Bury Club; while Slater, Lillywhite, King, and the Broadbridges, raised the name of Midhurst and of Sussex.

Against such batsmen every variety of underhand delivery failed to maintain the balance of the game, till J. Broadbridge and Lillywhite, after many protests and discussions, succeeded in establishing what long was called "the Sussex Bowling."

"About 1820," said Mr. Budd, "at our anniversary dinner (three-guinea tickets) at the Clarendon, Mr. Ward asked me if I had said I would play any man in England at single wicket, without fieldsmen. An affirmative produced a match p. p. for fifty guineas. On the day appointed Mr. Brand proved my opponent.

He was a fast bowler. I went in first, and, scoring seventy runs with some severe blows on the legs,—nankeen knees and silk stockings, and no pads in those days,—I consulted a friend and knocked down my own wicket, lest the match should last to the morrow, and I be unable to play. Mr. Brand was out without a run! I went in again, and making up the 70 to 100, I once more knocked down my own wicket, and once more my opponent failed to score!!

The flag was flying—the signal of a great match—and a large concourse were assembled, and considering Mr. Ward, a good judge, made the match, this is probably the most hollow beat on record.

Osbaldestone's victory was even more satisfactory. Lord Frederick with Beldham made a p. p. match with Osbaldestone and Lambert. "On the day named," said Budd, "I went to Lord Frederick, representing my friend was too ill to stand, and asked him to put off the match. "No; play or pay," said his Lordship, quite inexorable. "Never mind," said Osbaldestone, " I won't forfeit: Lambert may beat them both, and if he does the fifty guineas shall be his." I asked Lambert how he felt. "Why," said he, "they are anything but safe." His Lordship wouldn't hear of it. "Nonsense," he said, "you can't mean it." "Yes; play or pay, my Lord, we are in earnest, and shall claim the stakes!" and in fact Lambert did beat them both. For to play such a man when on his mettle was rather discouraging, and "he did make desperate exertion:" said Beldham, "Once he rushed up after his ball, and Lord Frederick was caught so near his bat that he lost his temper, and said it was not fair play. Of course, all hearts were with Lambert."

"Osbaldestone's mother sat by in her carriage, and enjoyed the match, and then," said Beldham, "Lambert was called to the carriage and bore away a paper parcel : some said it was a gold watch,—some, bank notes. Trust Lambert to keep his own secrets. We were all curious, but no one ever knew."

## CHAP. VI.

### A DARK CHAPTER IN THE HISTORY OF CRICKET.

THE lovers of cricket may congratulate themselves at the present day that matches are made at cricket, as at chess, rather for love and the honor of victory than for money.

It is now many years since Lord's was frequented by men with book and pencil, betting as openly and professionally as in the ring at Epsom, and ready to deal in the odds with any and every person of speculative propensities. Far less satisfactory was the state of things with which Lord F. Beauclerk and Mr. Ward had to contend, to say nothing of the earlier days of the Earl of Winchelsea and Sir Horace Mann. As to the latter period, "Old Nyren" bewails its evil doings. He speaks of one who had "the trouble of proving himself a rogue," and also of "the legs at Marylebone," who tried, for once in vain, to corrupt some primitive specimens of Hambledon innocence. He says, also, the grand matches of his day were always made for 500*l.* a side. Add to this the fact that the bets were in proportion, that Jim and Joe Bland, of turf notoriety, Dick Whitlom, of Covent Garden, Simpson, a gaming-house keeper, and Toll, of Isher, as regularly attended at a match as Crockford and Gully at Epsom and Ascot; and the idea that all the Surrey and Hampshire rustics should either want or resist strong temptations to sell is not to be entertained for a moment. The constant habit of betting will take the honesty out of any man. A half-crown sweepstakes, or betting such odds as lady's long kids to gentleman's short ditto, is all very fair sport; but if a man after years of high betting can still preserve the fine edge and tone of honest feeling, he is indeed a wonder. To bet on a certainty all admit is swindling. If so, to bet where you feel it a certainty must be very bad moral practice.

"If gentlemen wanted to bet," said Beldham, "just under the pavilion sat men ready with money down to give and take the current odds, and by far the best men to bet with, because if they lost it was all in the way of business: they paid their money and did not grumble." Still they had all sorts of tricks to make their betting safe. "One artifice," said Mr. Ward, "was to keep a player out of the way by a false report that his wife was dead." Then these men would come down to the Green Man and Still, and drink with us, and always said that those who backed us, or "the nobs," as they called them, sold the matches; and so, sir, as you are going the round beating up the quarters of the old players, you will find some to persuade you this is true. But don't believe it. That any gentleman, in my day, ever put himself into the power of these blacklegs by selling matches, I can't credit. Still, one day I thought I would try how far these tales were true. So, going down into Kent with "one of high degree," he said to me, "Will, if this match is won, I lose a hundred pounds." "Well," said I, "my Lord, you and I could order that." He smiled as if nothing were meant, and talked of something else; and, as luck would have it, he and I were in together, and brought up the score between us, though every run seemed to me like "a guinea out of his Lordship's pocket."

In those days foot races were very common. Lord Frederick and Mr. Budd were first-rate runners, and bets were freely laid. So, one day, old Fennex laid a trap for the gentlemen: he brought up to act the part of some silly conceited youngster, with his pockets full of money, a first-rate runner out of Hertfordshire. This soft young gentleman ran a match or two with some known third-rate men, and seemed to win by a neck, and no pace to spare. Then he calls out, "I'll run any man on the ground for 25*l*., money down." A match was quickly made, and money laid on pretty thick on Fennex's account. Some said, "Too bad to win of such a green young fellow;" others said, "He's old enough—serve him right." So the laugh was finely against those who were taken in; "the green one" ran away like a hare!

"You see, sir," said one fine old man, with brilliant eye and quickness of movement, that showed his right hand had not yet forgot its cunning, "matches were bought, and matches were sold, and gentlemen who meant honestly lost large sums of money, till the rogues beat themselves at last. They overdid it; they spoilt their own trade; and, as I told one of them, a knave and a fool makes a bad partnership: so, you and yourself will never prosper. Well, surely there was robbery enough, and not a few of the great players earned money to their own disgrace; but, if you'll believe me, there was not half the selling there was said to be. Yes, I can guess, sir, much as you have been talking to all the old players over this good stuff (pointing to the brandy and water I had provided,) no doubt you have heard that B —— sold as bad as the rest. I'll tell the truth: one match up the country I did sell,—a match made by Mr. Osbaldestone at Nottingham. I had been sold out of a match just before, and lost 10*l*., and happening to hear it I joined two others of our eleven to sell, and get back my money. I won 10*l*. exactly, and of this roguery no one ever suspected me; but many was the time I have been blamed for selling when as innocent as a babe. In those days when so much money was on the matches, every man who lost his money would blame some one. Then if A missed a catch, or B made no runs,—and where's the player whose hand is always in?—that man was called a rogue directly. So when a man was doomed to lose his character, and bear all the smart, there was the more temptation to do like others, and after 'the kicks' to come in for 'the halfpence.' But I am an old man now, and heartily sorry I have been ever since, because, but for that Nottingham match, I could have said, with a clear conscience, to a gentleman like you, that all that was said was false, and I never sold a match in my life; but now I can't. But if I had fifty sons, I would never put one of them, for all the games in the world, in the way of the roguery that I have witnessed. The temptation really was very great,—too great by far for any poor man to be exposed to,—no richer than ten shillings a week, let alone harvest time. I never told you the way I first was brought to London. I was a lad of eighteen at this Hampshire village, and Lord Winchelsea had seen us play among ourselves, and watched the match with the Hambledon Club on Broad-halfpenny, when I scored forty-three against David Harris, and ever so many of the runs against David's bowling, and no one ever could manage David before. So, next year, in the month of March, I was down in the meadows, when a gentleman came across the field with Farmer Hilton, and thought I, all in a minute, now this is something about cricket. Well, at last it was settled. I was to play Hampshire against England, at London, in White Conduit-Fields ground, in the month of June. For three months I did nothing but think about that match. Tom Walker was to travel up from this country, and I agreed to go with him, and found myself at last, with a merry company of cricketers, all old men, whose names I had ever heard as foremost in the game—met together, drinking, card-playing, betting, and singing at the Green Man (that was the great cricketer's house), in Oxford Street,—no man without his wine, I assure you, and such suppers as three guineas a game to lose, and five to win (that was then the pay for players) could never pay for long. To go to London by a waggon, earn five guineas three or four times told, and come back with half the money in your pocket to the plough again, was all very well talking. You know what young folk are, sir, when they get together: mischief brews stronger in large quantities: so many spent all their earnings, and were soon glad to make more money some other way. Hundreds of pounds were bet upon the great matches, and other wagers laid on the scores of the finest players, and that too by men who had a book for every race, and every match in the sporting world: men who lived by gambling; and as to honesty, gambling and honesty don't often go together. What was easier, then, than for such sharp gentlemen to mix with the players, take advantage of their difficulties, and say, your backers, my Lord this, and the Duke of that, sell matches and overrule all your good play, so why shouldn't you have a share of the plunder? That was their constant argument. Serve them as they serve you. You have heard of Jim Bland, the turfsman, and his brother Joe—two nice boys. When Jemmy Dawson was hanged for poisoning the horse, the Blands never felt safe till the rope was round Dawson's neck, and, to keep him quiet, persuaded him to the last hour that they dared not hang him: and a certain nobleman had a reprieve in his pocket. Well, one day in April, Joe Bland found me out in this parish, and tried his game on with me. 'You may make a fortune,' he said, 'if you will listen to me: so much for the match with Surrey, and so much more for the Kent match—' 'Stop,' said I: 'Mr. Bland, you talk too fast; I am rather too old for this trick; you never buy the same man but once: if their lordships ever sold at all, you would peach upon them if ever after they dared to win. You'll try me once, and then you'll have me in a line like him of the mill last year.' No, sir, a man was a slave when once he sold to these folk: fool and knave aye go together. Still they found fools enough for their purpose; but rogues can never trust each other. One day a sad quarrel arose between two of them; that opened the gentlemen's eyes too wide to close again to these practices. Two very big rogues at Lord's fell a quarrelling, and blows were given; a crowd drew round, and the gentlemen ordered them both into the pavilion. When the one began, 'You had 20l. to lose the Kent match, bowling leg long hops and missing catches.' 'And you were paid to lose at Swaffham—' Why did that game with Surrey turn about—three runs to get, and you didn't make them?' Angry words came out fast, and, when they are circumstantial and square with previous suspicions, they are proofs as strong as holy writ. In one single-wicket match," he continued, " and those were always great matches for the sporting men, because usually you had first-rate men on each side, and their merits known; dishonesty was as plain as this: just as a player was coming in (John B. will confess this, if you talk of the match) he said to me, ' You'll let me score five or six, for appearances, won't you, for I am not going to make many if I can?' ' Yes,' I said, ' you rogue, you shall, if I can *not* help it.' But when a game was all but won, and the odds heavy, and all one way, it was cruel to see how the fortune of the day then would change about. In that Kent match,—you can turn to it in your book (Bentley's scores), played 28th July, 1807, on Pennenden Heath,—I and Lord Frederick had scored sixty-one, and thirty remained to win, and six of the best men in England went out for eleven runs. Well, sir, I lost some money by that match, and as seven of us were walking homewards to meet a coach, a gentleman who had backed the match drove by and said, ' Jump up, my boys, we have all lost together. I need not mind if I hire a pair of horses extra next town, for I have lost money enough to pay for twenty pair or more.' Well, thought I, as I rode along, you have rogues enough in your carriage now, if the truth were told, I'll answer for it; and one of them let out the secret some ten years after. But, sir, I can't help laughing when I tell you, once there was a single-wicket match played at Lord's, and a man on each side was paid to lose. One was bowler, and the other batsman, when the game came to a near point. I knew their politics, the rascals, and saw in a minute how things stood; and how I did laugh, to be sure: for seven balls together, one would not bowl straight, and the other would not hit; but at last a straight ball must come, and down went the wicket."

From other information received, I could tell this veteran that, even in his much-repented Nottingham match, his was not the only side that had men resolved to lose. The match was sold for Nottingham too, and that with less success, for Nottingham won: an event the less difficult to accomplish, as Lord Frederick Beauclerk broke a finger in an attempt to stop a designed and wilful overthrow! and played the second innings with one hand.

It is true, Clarke, who played in the match, thought all was fair: still, he admits, he heard one Nottingham man accused on the field, by his own side, of foul play. This confirms the evidence of the Rev. C. W., no slight authority in Nottingham matches, who said he was cautioned before the match that all would not be fair.

"This practice of selling matches," said Beldham, "produced strange things sometimes. Once, I remember, England was playing Surrey, and, in my judgment, Surrey had the best side; still I found the Legs were betting seven to four against Surrey! This time they were done; for they betted on the belief that some Surrey men had sold the match, but Surrey played to win.

Crockford used to be seen about Lord's, and Mr. Gully also occasionally, but only for society of sporting men: they did not understand the game, and I never saw them bet. Mr. Gully was often talking to me about the game for one season; but I could never put any sense into him! He knew plenty about fighting, and afterwards of horse-racing; but a man cannot learn the odds of cricket unless he is something of a player."

## CHAP. VII.

#### THE SCIENCE AND ART OF BATTING.

A WRITER in "Blackwood" once attributed the success of his magazine to the careful exclusion of every bit of science, or reasoning, above half an inch long. The Cambridge Professors do not exclusively represent the mind of Parker's Piece, so away with the stiffness of analysis and the mysteries of science: the laws of dynamics might puzzle, and the very name of *physics* alarm, many an able-bodied cricketer; so, invoking the genius of our mother tongue, let us exhibit science in its more palatable form.

All the balls that can be bowled may, for all practical purposes, be reduced to a few simple classes, and plain rules given for all and each. There are what are called good balls, and bad balls. The former, good lengths, and straight, while puzzling to the eye; the latter, bad lengths, and wide, while easy to see and to hit.

But, is not a good hand and eye quite enough, with a little practice, without all this theory? Do you ignore the Pilches and the Parrs, who have proved famous hitters from their own sense alone? The question is not how many have succeeded, but how many more have failed. Cricket by nature is like learning from a village dame; it leaves a great deal to be untaught before the pupil makes a good scholar. If you have Caldecourt's, Bayley's, or Dakin's instructions, *vivâ voce*, why not on paper also? What though many excellent musicians do not know a note, every good musician will bear witness that the consequence of Nature's teaching is, that men form a vicious habit almost impossible to correct, a lasting bar to brilliant execution. And why? — because the piano or the violin leaves no dexterity or rapidity to spare. The muscles act freely in one way only, in every other way with loss of power. So with batting. A good ball requires all the power and energy of the man! And as with riding, driving, rowing, or every other exercise, it depends on a certain form, attitude, or position, whether this power be forthcoming or not.

The scope for useful instructions for *forming good habits of hitting before their place is pre-occupied with bad*—for "there's the rub"— is very great indeed. If Pilch, and Clarke, and Lillywhite, averaging fifty years each, are still indifferent to pace in bowling,— and if Mr. Ward, as late as 1844, scored forty against Mr. Kirwan's swiftest bowling, while some of the most active young men, of long experience in cricket, are wholly unequal to the task,— then is it undeniable that a batsman may form a certain invaluable habit, which youth and strength cannot always give, nor age and inactivity entirely take away.

The following are simple rules for forming correct habits of play; for adding the judgment of the veteran to the activity of youth, or putting an old head on young shoulders, and teaching the said young shoulders not to get in each other's way.

All balls that can be bowled are reducible to "length balls" and "not lengths."

*Not lengths* are the toss, the tice, the half volley, the long hop, and ground balls.

These are *not length balls*, not pitched at that critical length which puzzles the judgment as to whether to play forward or back, as will presently be explained. These are all "bad balls," and among good players considered certain hits, though, from the delusive confidence they inspire, sometimes they are bowled with success against the best players.

These *not lengths*, therefore, being the easiest to play, as requiring only hand and eye, but little judgment, are the best for a beginner to practise; so we will set the tyro in a proper position to play them with certainty and effect.

POSITION. — Look at any professional player, — observe how he stands and holds his bat. Much, very much, depends on position,— so look at the figure of

Pilch. This is substantially the attitude of every good batsman. Some think he should bend the right knee a little; but an anatomist reminds me that it is when the limb is straight that the muscles are relaxed, and most ready for sudden action. Various as attitudes appear to the casual observer, all coincide in the main points marked in the figure of Pilch in our frontispiece. For all good players,—

1st. Stand with the right foot just within the line; further in would limit the reach and endanger the wicket, and further out would endanger stumping.

2dly. All divide their weight between their two feet, though making the right leg more the pillar and support, the left being rather lightly placed, and more ready to move on, off, or forward, and this we will call the balance foot.

3dly. All stand as close as they can without being before the wicket, otherwise the bat cannot be upright, nor can the eye command a line from the bowler's hand.

4thly. All stand at guard as upright as is easy to them. We say easy, not to forbid a slight stoop,— the attitude of extreme caution. Height is a great advantage, "and a big man," says Dakin, "is foolish to make himself into a little man." If the eye is low you cannot have the commanding sight, nor, as players say, "see as much of the game," as if you hold up your head, and look well at the bowler.

5thly. All stand easy, and hold the bat lightly, yet firmly in their hands. However rigid your muscles, you must relax them, as already observed, before you can start into action. Rossi, the sculptor, made a beautiful marble statue of a batsman at guard, for the late Mr. William Ward, who said, "You are no cricketer, Mr. Sculptor; the wrists are too rigid, and hands too much clenched."

Such is your position at guard, and when I tell you what you have to do, you will readily understand the meaning of *fig.* 1., " Receiving the Ball," or " Preparing for Action," in the next page.

*Meet the ball with as full a bat as the case admits.* Consider the full force of this rule.

1st. *Meet the ball.* The bat must strike the ball, not the ball the bat. Even if you block, you can block hard, and the wrists may do a little, so with a good player this rule admits of no exception. Young players must not think I mean a flourish, but an exact movement of the bat only at the latest possible instant. In playing back to a bail ball, a good player meets the ball, and plays it with a resolute movement of arm and wrist. Pilch is not caught in the attitude of what some call Hanging guard, letting the ball hit his bat dead, once in a season.

2dly. *With a full bat.* A good player has never less wood than 21 inches by 4¼ inches before his wicket as he plays the ball, a bad player has rarely more than a

## STRAIGHT PLAY PUZZLES BOWLERS. 107

*Fig. 1.*

Preparing for Action.*

bat's width alone. Remember the old rule, to keep the left shoulder over the ball, and left elbow well up. Good players must avoid doing this in excess, and playing from leg to off across the line of the ball in

* The toes are too much before Wicket, and foot hardly within the crease. Foreshortening suits our illustration better than artistic effect.

their over care to keep the shoulder over it. Fix a bat by pegs in the ground, and try to bowl the wicket down, and you will perceive what an unpromising antagonist this simple rule creates. I like to see a bat, as the ball is coming, hang perpendicular as a pendulum from the player's wrists. The best compliment ever paid me was this. "Whether you play forward or back, hitting or stopping, the wicket is always covered to the full measure of your bat." So said a friend well known in North Devon, whose effective bowling, combined with his name, has so often provoked the pun of "the falls of the *Clyde.*"

Herein, then, consists the great excellence of batting, *in presenting the largest possible face of the bat to the ball.* While the bat is descending on the ball, the ball may rise or turn, to say nothing of the liability of the hand to miss, and then the good player has always half the width of his bat, besides its height, to cover the deviation, whereas the cross player may err not only from the inaccuracy of hand and eye, but from the twist of the ball.

And would you bring a full bat even to a toss? Would you not cut it to the off or hit across to the on?

This question tries my rule very hard, certainly; but though nothing less than a hit from a toss can satisfy a good player, still I have seen the most brilliant hitters, when a little out of practice, lose their wicket, or hit a catch from the edge of the bat, by this common custom of hitting across even to a toss or long hop.

To hit tosses is good practice, requiring good time and quick wrist play. If you see a man play stiff, and "up in a heap," a swift toss is worth trying. Bowlers should practise both toss and tice.

We remember Wenman playing well against fine bowling; an underhand bowler was put on, who bowled him with a toss, fourth ball.

To play tosses, and ground balls, and hops, and every variety of loose bowling, by the rigid rules of straight and upright play, is a principle by which the old hands have often had a laugh at the young ones. Often have I been amused to see the wonder and disappointment occasioned, when some noted member of a University Eleven, or the Marylebone Club, from whom all expected, of course, the most tremendous hitting off "mere underhand bowling," has been easily disposed of by a toss or a ground ball, yclept a "sneak."

A fast ball to the middle stump, however badly bowled, no player can afford to treat too easily. A ball that grounds more than once may turn more than once, and the bat, though properly $4\frac{1}{4}$ inches wide, is considerably reduced when used across wicket; so *never hit across wicket*. To turn to loose bowling, and hit from leg stump square to the on side with full swing of the body, is very gratifying and very effective, and perhaps you may hit over the tent, or, as I once saw, into a neighbor's carriage; but while the natives are marvel-stricken, Caldecourt will shake his head, and inwardly grieve at folly so triumphant.

This reminds me of a memorable match in 1834, of Oxford against Cowley, the village which fostered those useful members of university society, who, during the summer term, bowl at sixpences on stumps, sometimes eight hours a day, and have strength enough left at the end to win one sixpence more.

The Oxonians, knowing the ground, or knowing their bowlers, scored above 200 runs in their first innings. Then Cowley grew wiser; and even now a Cowley man will tell the tale how they put on one Tailor Humphreys to bowl twisting underhand sneaks, at which the Oxonians laughed, and called it "no cricket;" but it actually levelled their wickets for fewer runs than were made against Bayley and Cobbett the following week. The Oxonians, too eager to score, and thinking it so easy, hit across, and did not play their usual game.

Never laugh at bowling that takes wickets. Bowling that is bad, often, for that very reason, meets with batting that is worse. Nothing shows a thorough player more than playing with caution even badly pitched underhand bowling.

One of the best judges of the game I ever knew was once offered by a fine hitter a bet that he could not, with his underhand bowling, make him " give a chance" in half an hour.

"Then you know nothing of the game," was the reply; "I would bowl you nothing but off tosses, which you must cut; you would not cut those correctly for half an hour, for you could not use a straight bat once. Your bet ought to be,—no chance before so many runs."

Peter Heward, an excellent wicket-keeper of Leicester,—of the same day as Henry Davis, one of the finest and most graceful hitters ever seen, as Dakin or any midland player will attest,—once observed to me, "Players are apt to forget that a bad bowler may bowl one or two balls as well as the best; so to make a good average you must always play the same guarded and steady game, and take care especially when late in the season." "Why late in the season?" "Because the ground is damp and heavy—it takes the spring out of good bowling, and gives fast underhand bowling as many twists as it has hops, besides making it hang in the ground. This game is hardly worth playing, it is true; but a man is but half a player who is only prepared for true ground." "We do not play cricket," he continued, "on billiard tables; wind and weather and the state of the turf make all the difference. So, if you play to win, play the game that will carry you through, and that is a straight and upright game; use your eyes well; play not at the pitch, nor by the length, but always (what few men do) at the ball itself, and never hitting across wicket."

Next as to the *half-volley*. This is the most delightful of all balls to hit, because it takes the right part of the bat, with all the quickness of its rise or rebound. Any player will show you what a half-volley is, and I presume that every reader has some living lexicon to explain common terms. A half-volley, then, is very generally hit in the air, soaring far above every fieldsman's head; and to know the power of the bat, every hitter should learn so to hit at pleasure. Though as a rule, *high hits make a low average*. But I am now to speak only of hitting half-volleys along the ground.

Every time you play forcibly at the pitch of a ball you have more or less of the half-volley; so this is a material point in batting. The whole secret consists partly in timing your hit well, and partly in taking the ball at the right part of the rise, so as to play the ball down without wasting its force against the ground.

Every player thinks he can hit a half-volley along the ground; but if once you see it done by a really brilliant hitter, you will soon understand that such hitting admits of many degrees of perfection. You will also see that there is a certain way of feeling the ball on the bat, while you spring it away with an elastic impulse; also, when the ball is quite within your reach, there is a certain smartness of hitting, the bat appearing to be loosely flung upon the ball, producing an astonishing effect; for, the ball appears not so much hit as shot away, with such speed as defies the fieldsman to cover it.

Clean hitting requires a loose arm, the bat held firmly, but not clutched in the hand; clumsy gloves are a sad hindrance, the hit is not half so crisp and smart; the bat must be brought forward not only by the free swing of the arm working well from the shoulder, but also by the wrist. (Refer to *fig.* 1. p. 107.) Here is the bat ready thrown back, and wrists proportionally bent; from that position a hit is always assisted by wrists as well as arm. The effect of the wrist alone, slight as its power appears, is very material in hitting; this probably arises from the greater precision and better time in which a wrist hit is commonly made.

As to hard hitting, if two men have equal skill, the strong man will strike the harder blow. Many slight men drive a ball nearly as far as larger men, because they exert their force in a more skilful manner. We have seen a man six feet three inches in height, and of power in proportion, hit a ball tossed to him—not once or twice, but repeatedly—a hundred yards or more in the air. This, perhaps, is more than any light man could do. But "the best man at putting the stone and throwing a weight," observes a friend, "I ever saw, was a man of little more than ten stone. The application of a man's whole weight at the proper moment is the chief point in this as in wrestling, and so also is hard hitting."

The whirl of the bat may be accelerated by wrist, forearm, and shoulder, let each joint bear its proper part.

NUTS FOR STRONG TEETH.—All effective hits must be made with both hands and arms; and, in order that both arms may apply their force, the point at which the object aimed at is struck should be opposite the middle of the body.

Take a bat in your hand, poise the body as for a volley hit forward, the line from shoulder to shoulder being parallel with the line of the ball. Now whirl the bat in the line of the ball, and you will find that it reaches that part of its circle where it is perpendicular to the ground,—midway between the shoulders; at that moment, the bat attains its greatest velocity, so then alone can the strongest hit be made. Moreover, a hit made at this moment, will drive the ball parallel to and skimming the ground. And if, in such a hit, the lower six inches of the bat's face strike the ball, the hit is properly called a "clean hit," being free from all imperfections. The same may be said of a horizontal hit, or cut. The bat should meet the ball when opposite the body. I do not say that every hit should be made in this manner; I only say that a perfect hit can be made in no other, and that it should be the aim of the batsman to attain this position of the body as often as he can. Nor is this mere speculation on the scientific principle of batting; it arises from actual observation of the movements of the best batsmen. All really good hitters make their hits just at the moment when the ball is opposite the middle of their body. Watch any fine off hitter. If he hits to mid-wicket, his breast is turned to mid-wicket; if he hits, I mean designedly, to point, his breast is turned to point. I do not say that his hits would always go to those parts of the field because the speed and spin of the ball will always, to a greater or less degree, prevent its going in the precise direction of the hit; but I only say that the ball is always hit by the best batsmen when just opposite to them. Cutting forms no exception: the best cutters turn the body round on the basis of the feet till the breast fronts the ball,—having let the ball go almost as far as the bails,—and then the full power of the hitter is brought to bear with the least possible diminution of the original speed of the ball. This is the meaning of the observation,—that fine cutters appear to follow the ball, and at the latest moment cut the ball off the bails; for, if you do not follow the ball, by turning your breast to it at the moment you hit, you can have no power for a fine cut. It makes good "chamber practice" to suspend a ball oscillating by a string: you will soon see wherein lies the peculiar power of cutting, which characterizes Mr. Bradshaw, Mr. Felix, and Mr. C. Taylor; as of old, Searle, Saunders, and Robinson. Robinson cut so late that the ball often appeared past the wicket.

And these hints will suffice to awaken attention to the powers of the bat. Clean hitting is a thing to be carefully studied; the player who has never discovered his deficiency in it, had need examine and see whether there is not a secret he has yet to learn.

*The Tice.* Safest to block: apt to be missed, because a dropping ball; hard to get away, because on the ground. Drop the bat smartly on the ground, and it will make a run, but do not try too much of a hit. The Tice is almost a full pitch; the way to hit it, says Caldecourt, is to go in and make it a full pitch: I cannot advise this for beginners. Going in even to a Tice puts you out of form for the next ball, and creates a dangerous habit.

*Ground balls*, and all balls that touch the ground more than once between wickets, I have already hinted, are reckoned very easy, but they are always liable to come in very dangerous. Sometimes you have three hops, and the last like a good length ball: they are liable to twist both on and off with the inequalities of the ground; also, if bowled with the least bias, there is much scope for that bias to produce effect. All these peculiarities account for the often puzzling fact that the best batsmen are out with the worst bowling. Bad bowling requires a game of its own, and a game of the greatest care, where too commonly we find the least, because " only underhand bowling, not by any means good lengths;" it requires especially playing at the ball itself, even to the last inch, and not by calculation of the pitch and rise.

Let me further remark that hitting, to be either free, quick, or clean, must be done by the arms and wrists, and not by the body, yet the weight of the body must be thrown in at the proper moment by putting down the left leg. Take it as a rule in hitting, that that which is not elegant is not right; for the human frame is rarely inelegant in its movements when all the muscles act in their natural direction. Many men play with their shoulders up to their ears, and their sinews all in knots, and because they are conscious of desperate exertion, they forget that their force is going anywhere than into the ball. It is an old saying, that hard hitting does not depend on strength. No. It depends not on the strength a man has, but on the strength he brings to bear; and strength is exerted in hitting, as in throwing a ball, in exact proportion to the rapidity of the whirl or circle which the bat or hand describes. The point of the bat moves faster in the circle than any other part, and, therefore, did not the jar, resulting from the want of resistance, place the point of hitting, as experience shows, a little higher up, the nearer the end the harder would be the hit. The wrist, however slight its force, acting with a multiplying power, adds greatly to the speed of this whirl.

Hard hitting, then, depends, first, on the freedom with which the arm revolves from the shoulder, unimpeded by constrained efforts and contortions of the body; next on the play of the arm at the elbow; thirdly, on the wrists. Observe any cramped, clumsy hitter, and you will recognize these truths at once. His elbow is glued to his side, his shoulder stiff at the joint, and the little speed of his bat depends on a twist and a wriggle of his whole body.

Keep your body as composed and easy as the requisite adjustment of the left leg will admit; let your arms do the hitting; and remember the wrists. The whiz that meets the ear will be a criterion of increasing power. Practise hard hitting,—that is, the full and timely application of your strength, not only for the value of the extra score, but because hard hitting and correct and clean hitting are one and the same thing. Mere stopping balls and poking about in the blockhole is not cricket, however successful; and I must admit, that one of the most awkward, poking, vexatious blockers that ever produced a counterfeit of cricket, defied Bayley and Cobbett at Oxford in 1836,—three hours, and made five and thirty runs. Another friend, a better player, addicted to the same teasing game, in a match at Exeter in 1845, blocked away till his party, the N. Devon, won the match, chiefly of byes and wide balls! Such men might have turned their powers to much better account.

Some maintain that anything that succeeds is cricket; but not such cricket as full-grown men should vote a scientific and a manly exercise; otherwise, to "run cunning" might be Coursing, and to kill sitting Shooting. A player may happen to succeed with what is not generally a successful style,—winning in spite of his awkwardness, and not by virtue of it.

But there is another cogent reason for letting your arms, and not your body, do the work,— namely, that it makes all the difference to your sight whether the level of the eye remains the same as with a composed and easy hitter, or unsteady and changing, as with the wriggling and the clumsy player. Whether a ball undulates in the air, or whether there is an equal undulation in the line of the eye which regards that ball, the confusion and indistinctness is exactly the same. Look at any distant object, and wave your head up and down for an experiment, and you will understand the confusion of sight to which I allude. The only security of a good batsman, as of a good shot, consists in the hand and eye being habituated to act together. Now the hand may obey the eye when at rest, but have no such habit when in unsteady motion. And this shows how uncertain all hitting must be, when, either by the movement of the body or other cause, the line of sight is suddenly raised or depressed.

The same law of sight shows the disadvantage of men who stand at guard very low, and then suddenly raise themselves as the ball is coming.

The same law of sight explains the disadvantage of

stepping in to hit, especially a slow dropping ball: the eye is puzzled by a double motion—the change in the level of the ball, and the change in the level of the line of sight.

So much for our theory—now for experience. Look at Pilch and all fine players!

How characteristic is the ease and repose of their figures — no hurry or trepidation. How little do their heads or bodies move! Whereas bad players move a dozen times while the ball is coming, as if they stood on a hot iron, with precisely the disadvantage that attends an unsteady telescope. "Then you would actually teach a man how to see?" We would teach him how to give his eyes a fair chance. Of sight, as of quickness, most players have enough, if they would only make good use of it.

To see a man wink his eyes and turn his head away is not uncommon the first day of partridge shooting, and quite as common at the wicket. An undoubting judgment and knowledge of the principles of batting literally improves the sight, for it increases that calm confidence which is essential for keeping your eyes open and in a line to see clearly.

Sight of a ball also depends on a habit of undivided attention both before and after delivery.

## A HABIT OF STRAIGHT AND UPRIGHT PLAY.

To be a good judge of a horse, to have good common sense, and to hit straight and upright at Cricket, are qualifications never questioned without dire offence. Yet few, very few, ever play as upright as they might play, and that even to guard their three stumps. To be able, with a full and upright bat, to play well over and command a ball a few inches to the Off, or a little to the leg, is a very superior and rare order of ability.

The first exercise for learning upright play is to practise several times against an easy bowler, with both hands on the same side of the handle of the bat. Not that this is the way to hold a bat in play, though the bat so held must be upright; but this exercise of rather poking than playing will insure you to the habit and method of upright play. Afterwards, shift your hands to their proper position, and practise slipping your left hand round into the same position, while in the act of coming forward.

But be sure you stand up to your work, or close to your block-hole; and let the bowler admonish you every time you shrink away or appear afraid of the ball. Much practice is required before it is possible for a young player to attain that perfect composure and indifference to the ball that characterizes the professor.

The least nervousness or shrinking is sure to draw the bat out of the perpendicular. As to shrinking from the ball—I do not mean any apprehension of injury, but only the result of a want of knowledge of length or distance, and the result of uncertainty as to how the ball is coming, and how to prepare to meet it. Nothing distinguishes the professor from the amateur, more than the composed and unshrinking posture in which he plays a ball.

Practice alone will prevent shrinking: encouraging your bowler continually reminds you of it. As to practising with a bowler, you see some men at Lord's and the University grounds batting hour after hour, as if cricket were to be taken by storm. To practise long at one time is positively injurious. For about one hour a man may practise to advantage; for a second hour he may rather improve his batting even by keeping wicket, or being long stop. Anything is good practice for batting that habituates the hand and eye to act together.

The next exercise is of a more elegant kind, and quite coincident with your proper game. Always throw back the point of the bat, while receiving the ball, to the top of the middle stump, as in figure, page 107; then the handle will point to the bowler, and the whole bat be in the line of the wicket. By commencing in this position, you cannot fail to bring your bat straight and full upon the ball. If you take up your bat straight, you cannot help hitting straight; but, if once you raise the point of the bat across the wicket, to present a full bat for that ball is quite impossible.

One advantage of this exercise is that it may be practised even without a bowler. The path of a field, with ball and bat, and a stick for a stump, are all the appliances required. Place the ball before you, one, two, or more feet in advance, and more or less On or Off, at discretion. Practise hitting with right foot always fixed, and with as upright and full a bat as possible: keep your left elbow up, and always over the ball.

This exercise will teach, at the same time, the full powers of the bat; what style of hitting is most efficacious; at what angle you smother the ball, and at what you can hit clean; only, be careful to play in form; and always see that your right foot has not moved before you follow to pick up the ball. Fixing the right foot is alone a great help to upright play; for, while the right foot remains behind, the right shoulder cannot come forward; and this it must do to hit across wicket. Firmness in the right foot is also essential to hard hitting, for you cannot exert much strength, unless you stand in a firm and commanding position.

Upright and straight hitting, then, requires, briefly, the point of the bat thrown back to the middle stump as the ball is coming; secondly, the left elbow well up; and, thirdly, the right foot fixed, and near the blockhole.

Never play a single ball without strict attention to these three rules. At first, you will feel cramped and powerless; but practice will soon give ease and elegance; and you will have mastered the principle, not only of all sure defence, but of all certain hitting; for the straight player has always wood enough and to spare in the way of the ball; whereas, the deviation of half an inch leaves the cross-player at fault. Mr. William Ward once played a single wicket match with a thick stick, against another with a bat; yet these are not much more than the odds of good straight play against cross play. At Cheltenham College, the first Eleven plays the second Eleven "a broomstick match." From the 400 pupils and masters an Eleven is chosen superior to any in the county of Gloucester; and I venture to predict that Mr. M. K. will be among the first players in Cambridge, and raise Cheltenham high among the schools of cricketers.

When a player hits almost every time he raises his bat, the remark is, What an excellent eye that batsman has! But upright play tends far more than eye to certainty in hitting. It is not easy to miss when you make the most of every inch of your bat. But when you trust to the width alone, a slight error produces a miss, and not uncommonly a catch.

The great difficulty in learning upright play consists in detecting when you are playing across. So your practice-bowler must remind you of the slightest shifting of the foot, shrinking from the wicket, or declination of your bat. Straight bowling is more easy to stand up to without nervous shrinking, and slow bowling best reveals every weak point, because a slow ball must be played: it will not play itself. Many a stylish player is beat by slow bowling, because never thoroughly grounded in the principles of correct play and judgment of lengths.

Underhand bowling is the best of any for a learner, and learners are, or should be, a large class. Being generally at the wicket, it produces the straightest play: falling stumps are "no flatterers, but feelingly remind us what we are." Caldecourt, who had a plain, though judicious, style of bowling, once observed a weak point in Mr. Ward's play, and levelled his stumps three times in about as many balls. Many men, boasting, as Mr. Ward then did, of nearly the first average of his day, would have blamed the bowler, the ground, the wind, and, in short, any thing but themselves; but Mr. Ward, a liberal patron of the game, in the days of his prosperity, gave Caldecourt a guinea for his judgment in the game and his useful lesson. "Such," Dr. Johnson would say, "is the spirit and self-denial of those whose memories are not doomed to decay" with their bats, but play cricket for "immortality."

### PLAYING FORWARD AND BACK.

We have now to speak of playing length-balls, and when to play forward at the pitch of the ball, and when back for better sight of the rebound.

A length-ball is one that pitches at a puzzling length from the bat. This is a length that cannot be reduced to measurement, depending on the delivery of the bowler and the reach of the batsman.

Any ball is a length-ball which pitches almost, but not quite, within the command of a batsman, according to his reach and ability. For more intelligible explanation, I must refer you to your friends.

Every player is conscious of one particular length that puzzles him,—of one point between himself and the bowler, in which he would rather that the ball should not pitch. "There is a length-ball that almost blinds you," said an experienced player at Lord's. There is a length that makes many a player shut his eyes and turn away his head. "A length," says Mr. Felix, "that brings over a man most indescribable emotions." There are two ways to play such balls; to discriminate is difficult, and, "if you doubt, you are lost." Let A be the furthest point

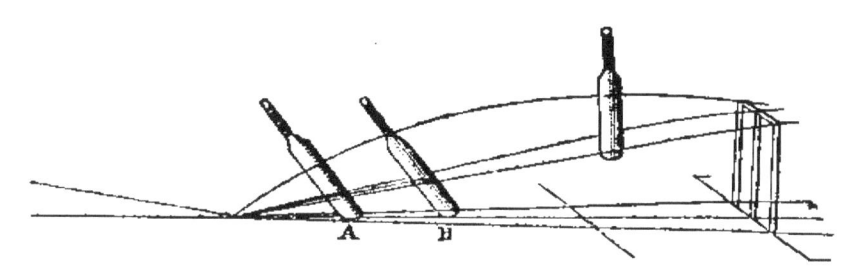

to which a good player can reach, so as to plant his bat at the proper angle, at once preventing a catch, stopping a shooter, and intercepting a bailer. Then, at any point short of A, should the bat be placed, the ball may rise over the bat if held to the ground, or shoot under if the bat is a little raised. At B the same single act of planting the bat cannot both cover a bailer and stop a shooter. Every ball which the batsman can reach, as at A, may be met with a full bat forward; and, being taken at the pitch, it is either stopped or driven away with all its rising, cutting, shooting, or twisting propensities undeveloped. But any ball you cannot cover, as at B, must be played back nearly in the attitudes shown in pages 107, and 141. This back play gives as long a sight of the ball as possible, and enables the player either to be up for a bailer or down for a shooter.

MORE HARD NUTS.—Why do certain lengths puzzle, and what is the nature of all this puzzling emotion? It is a sense of confusion and of doubt. At the moment of the pitch, the ball is lost in the ground; so you doubt whether it will rise, or whether it will shoot—whether it will twist, or come in straight. The eye follows the ball till it touches the ground: till this moment there is no great doubt, for its course is known to be uniform. I say no great doubt, because there is always some doubt till the ball has passed some yards from the bowler's hand. The eye cannot distinguish the direction of a ball approaching, till it has seen a fair portion or a good sample of the flight of it. Then only can you calculate what the rest of the flight will be. Still, before the ball has pitched, the first doubt is resolved, and the batsman knows the ball's direction; but, when once it touches the ground, the change of light alone (earth instead of air being the back ground) is trying to the eye. Then at the rise recommences all the uncertainty of a second delivery; for the direction of the ball has once more to be ascertained, and that requires almost as much time for sight as will sometimes bring the ball into the wicket.

All this difficulty of sight applies only to the batsman; to him the ball is advancing and foreshortened in proportion as it is straight. If the ball is rather wide, or if seen, as by Point, from the side, the ball may be easily traced, without confusion, from first to last. It is the fact of an object approaching perfectly straight to you, that confuses your sense of distance. Thus, a man standing on a railway cannot judge of the nearness of the engine; nor a man behind a target of the approach of the arrow. Though seen obliquely, the flight is clear. A long hop is not a puzzling length, because there is time to ascertain the second part of the course or rebound: a toss is easy, because one course only. The tice also, and the half-volley, or any over-pitched ball, are not so puzzling, because they may be met forward, and thus the two parts of the flight reduced to one. Such is the philosophy of forward play, intended to obviate the batsman's chief difficulty, which is with the second part or the rebound of the ball.

The following are good rules :—

1. Meet every ball at the pitch by forward play which you can conveniently cover.

Whatever ball you can play forward, you can play safely—as by one single movement. But in playing the same ball back, you give yourself two things to think of instead of one—stopping and keeping down a bailer, and stopping a shooter. Every ball is the more difficult to play back in exact proportion to the ease with which it might be played forward. The player has a shorter sight, and less time to see the nature of the rise; so the ball crowds upon him, affording neither time nor space for effective play. Never play back but of necessity; meet every ball forward which you can conveniently cover—I say *conveniently*, because, if the pitch of the ball cannot be reached without danger of losing your balance, misplacing your bat, or drawing your foot out of your ground, that ball should be considered out of reach, and be played back. This rule many fine players, in their eagerness to score, are apt to violate; so, if the ball rises abruptly, they are bowled or caught. There is also danger of playing wide of the ball, if you over-reach.

2. Some say, when in doubt, play back. Certainly all balls may be played back; but many it is almost impracticable to play forward. But since the best forward players may err, the following hint, founded on the practice of Fuller Pilch, will suggest an excellent means of getting out of a difficulty:—Practise the art of *half-play*; that is, practise going forward to balls a little beyond your reach, and then, instead of planting your bat near the pitch, which is supposed too far distant to be effectually covered, watch for the ball about half-way, being up if it rises, and down if it shoots. By this half-play, which I learnt from one of Pilch's pupils, I have often saved my wicket when I found myself forward for a ball out of reach; though before, I felt defenceless, and often let the ball pass either under or over my bat. Still half-play, though a fine saving clause for proficients, is but a choice of evils, and no practice for learners, as forming a bad habit. By trying too many ways, you spoil your game.

3. Ascertain the extent of your utmost reach for-

ward, and practise accordingly. The simplest method is to fix your right foot at the crease, and try how far forward you can conveniently plant your bat at the proper angle; then, allowing that the ball may be covered at about three feet from its pitch, you will see at once how many feet you can command in front of the crease. Pilch could command from ten to twelve feet. Some short men will command ten feet; that is to say, they will safely meet forward every ball pitching within that distance from the crease.

There are two ways of holding a bat in playing forward. The position of the hands, as of Pilch, in the frontispiece, standing at guard, will not admit of a long reach forward. But by shifting the left hand behind the bat, the action is free, and the reach unimpeded.

Every learner must practise this shifting of the left hand in forward play. The hand will soon come round naturally. Also learn to reach forward with composure and no loss of balance. Play forward evenly and gracefully, with rather an elastic movement. Practice will greatly increase your reach. Take care you do not lose sight of the ball, as many do, and look at the ball itself, not merely at the spot where you expect it to pitch. Much depends on commencing at the proper moment, and not being in a hurry. More useful hints on forward play are found in our last pages.

Forward play may be practised almost as well in a room as in a cricket-field : better still with a ball in the path of a field. To force a ball back to the bowler or long-field by hard forward play is commonly called Driving; and driving you may practise without any bowler, and greatly improve in balance and correctness of form, and thus increase the extent of your reach, and habituate the eye to a correct discernment of the point at which forward play ends and back play begins. By practice you will attain a power of coming forward with a spring, and playing hard or driving. All fine players drive nearly every ball they meet forward, and this driving admits of so many degrees of strength that sometimes it amounts to quite a hard hit. "I once," said Clarke, "had thought there might be a school opened for cricket in the winter months, for you may drill a man to use a bat as well as a broadsword." With driving, as with half-play, be not too eager—play forward surely and steadily at first, otherwise the point of the bat will get in advance, or the hit be badly timed, and give a catch to the bowler. This is one error into which the finest forward players have sometimes gradually fallen—a vicious habit, formed from an overweening confidence and success upon their own ground. Comparing notes lately with an experienced player, we both remembered a time in which we thought we could make hard and free hits even off those balls which good players play gently back to the bowler; but eventually a succession of short innings sent us back to safe and sober play.

Sundry other hits are made, contrary to every rule, by players accustomed to one ground, or one set of bowlers. Many an Etonian has found that a game, which succeeded in the shooting fields, has proved an utter failure when all was new at Lord's, or in a country match.

Every player should practise occasionally with professional bowlers, for they look to the principle of play, and point out radical errors even in showy hits.

One great difficulty, we observed, consists in correct discrimination of length and instantaneous decision. To form correctly as the ball pitches, there is time enough, but none to spare: time only to act, no time to think. So also with shooting, driving, and various kinds of exercises, at the critical moment all depend not on thought, but habit; by constant practice, the time requisite for deliberation becomes less and less, till at length we are unconscious of any deliberation at all,—acting, as it were, by intuition or instinct, for the occasion prompts the action : then, in common language, we "do it naturally," or "have formed the habit of doing so."

In this sense a player must form a habit of correct decision in playing forward and back. Till he plays by habit he is not safe : the sight of the length must prompt the corresponding movement. Look at Fuller Pilch, or Mr. C. Taylor, and this rule will be readily understood ; for, with such players, every ball is as naturally and instinctively received by its appropriate movement as if the player were automaton, and the ball touched a spring : so quickly does forward play, or back, and the attitude for off cut or leg hit, appear to coincide with, or rather to anticipate, each suitable length. All this quickness, ease, and readiness marks a habit of correct play; and the question is how to form such a habit.

All the calmness and composure we admire in proficients results from a habit of playing each length in one way, and in one way only. To attain this habit, measure your reach before the crease as you begin to practise with a bowler, and make a mark visible to the bowler, but not such as will divert your own eye.

Having fixed such a mark, let your bowler pitch, as nearly as he can, sometimes on this side of the mark, sometimes on that. After every ball, you have only to ask which side? and you will have demonstrative proof whether your play has been right or wrong. Constant practice, with attention to the pitch, will habituate your eye to lengths, and enable you to decide in a moment how to play.

For my own part, I have rarely practised for years without this mark. It enables me to ascertain, by referring to the bowler, where any ball has pitched. To know at a glance the exact length of a ball, however necessary, is not quite as easy to the batsman as to the bowler; and, without practising with a mark, you may remain a long time in error.

After a few days' practice, you will become as certain of the length of each ball, and of your ability to reach it, as if you actually saw the mark, for you will carry the measurement in " your mind's eye."

So far well : you have gained a perception of lengths and distance; the next thing is to apply this knowledge. Therefore bear in mind you have a habit to form. No doubt many will laugh at this philosophy. Pilch does not know the " theory of moral habits," I dare say; but he knows well enough that wild practice spoils play; and if to educated men I please to say that wild play involves the formation of a set of bad habits to hang about you, and continually interfere with good intentions, where is the absurdity? How should you like to be doomed to play with some mischievous fellow, always tickling your elbow, and making you spasmodically play forward, when you ought to play back, or hit round, or cut when you ought to play straight? Precisely such a mischievous sprite is a bad habit. Till you have got rid of him, he is always liable to come across you, and tickle you out of your innings: all your resolution is no good. Habit is a much stronger principle than resolution. Accustom the hand to obey sound judgment, otherwise it will follow its old habit instead of your new principles.

To borrow an admirable illustration from Plato, which Socrates' pupil remarked was rather apt than elegant,—" While habit keeps up itching, man can't help scratching." And what is most remarkable in bad habits of play is, that long after a man thinks he has overcome them, by some chance association the old trick appears again, and a man feels (oh! fine for a moralist!) one law in his mind, and another law — or rather, let us say, he feels a certain latent spring in him ever liable to be touched, and disturb all the harmony of his cricketing economy.

Having, therefore, a habit to form, take the greatest pains that you methodically play forward to the overpitched and back to the underpitched balls. My custom was, the moment the ball pitched, to say audibly to myself, "forward," or "back." By degrees I was able to calculate the length sooner and sooner before the pitch, having, of course, the more time to prepare, till at last no sooner was the ball out of the bowler's hand, than ball and bat were visibly preparing for each other's reception. After some weeks' practice, forward and back play became so easy that I ceased to think about it, the very sight of the ball naturally suggesting the appropriate movement; in other words, I had formed a habit of correct play in this particular.

"*Dulci mari magno,*" says Lucretius; that is, it is delightful, from the vantage ground of science, to see others floundering in a sea of error, and to feel a happy sense of comparative security; — so was it no little pleasure to see the many wickets that fall, or the many catches that were made, from defects I had entirely overcome.

For, without the habit aforesaid, a man will often shut his eyes, remove his right fingers, as if the bat were too hot, and then look behind him and find his wicket down. A second will advance a foot forward, feel and look all abroad, and then try to seem unconcerned, if no mischief happens. A third will play back with the shortest possible sight of the ball, and hear his stumps rattle before he has time to do anything. A fourth will stand still, a fixture of fuss and confusion, with the same result; while a fifth will go gracefully forward, with straightest possible bat, and the most meritorious elongation of limb, and the ball will pass over the shoulder of his bat, traverse the whole length of his arms, and back, and colossal legs, tipping off the bails, or giving a chance to the wicket-keeper. Then, as Poins says of Falstaff, "The virtue of this jest will be the incomprehensible lies that this same fat rogue will tell us." For when a man is out by this simple error in forward or backward play, it would take a volume to record the variety of his excuses.

The reason so much has been said about habit is, partly, that the player may understand that bad habits are formed as readily as good; that a repetition of wild hits, or experimentalizing with hard hits off good lengths, may disturb your quick perception of critical lengths, and give you an uncontrollable habit of dangerous hitting.

THE SHOOTER.—This is the surest and most destructive ball that is bowled; stopping shooters depends on correct position and knowledge of the game.

The great thing is decision; to doubt is to lose time, and to lose time is to lose your wicket. And this decision requires a correct habit of forward and back play. But, since prevention is better than cure, by meeting at the pitch every ball within your reach, you directly diminish the number, not only of shooters, but of the most dangerous of all shooters, because those which afford the shortest time to play. But supposing you cannot cover the ball at the pitch, and a shooter it must be, then —

The first thing is to have the bat always pointed back to the bails, as in *fig.* 1, page 107; thus you will drop down on the ball, and have all the time and space the case admits of. If the bat is not thus thrown back, when the ball shoots the player has two operations,— the one to put the bat back, and the other to ground it, instead of one simple drop down alone. I never saw any man do this better than Wenman, when playing the North and South match at Lord's, in 1836. Redgate was in his prime, and almost all his balls were shooting down the hill; and, from the good time and precision with which Wenman dropped down upon some dozen shooters, with all the pace and spin for which Redgate was famous — the ground being hardened into brick by the sun — I have ever considered Wenman equal to any batsman of his day.

The second thing is, to prepare for back play with the first possible intimation that the ball will require it. A good player descries the enemy, and drops back as soon as the ball is out of the bowler's hand.

The third — a golden rule for batsmen — is: expect a good length to shoot, and you will have time, if it rises; but if you expect it to rise, you are too late if it shoots.

THE BAIL BALL.—First, the attitude is that of *fig.* 1. The bat thrown back to the bails is indispensable for quickness: if you play a bailer too late, short slip is placed on purpose to catch you out; therefore watch the ball from the bowler's hand, and drop back on your wicket in good time. Also, take the greatest pains in tracing the ball every inch from the hand to the bat.

Look hard for the twist, or a "break" will be fatal. To keep the eye steadily on the ball, and not lose it at the pitch, is a hint even for experienced players: so make this a subject for attentive practice.

The most difficult of all bailers are those which ought not to be allowed to come in as bailers at all, but be met at the pitch. Such overpitched balls give neither time nor space for safe play.

Every length ball is difficult to play back just in proportion to the ease with which it could be covered forward. A certain space, from nine to twelve feet, before the crease is, to a practised batsman, so much *terra firma*, whereon pitching every ball is a safe stop or score. Practise with the chalk mark, and learn to make this *terra firma* as wide as possible.

The DRAW is so called, I suppose, because, when perfectly made, there is no draw in it. Look at *fig.* 2. The bat is not drawn across the wicket, but hangs perpendicularly from the wrists; though the wrists of a good player are never idle, but bring the bat to meet the ball a few inches, and the hit is the natural angle formed by the opposing forces. "Say also," suggests Clarke, with his usual shrewd discernment, "that the ball meeting the bat, held easy in the hand, will turn it a little of its own force, and the wrists *feel* when to help it."

The Draw is the spontaneous result of straight play

## THE DRAW.

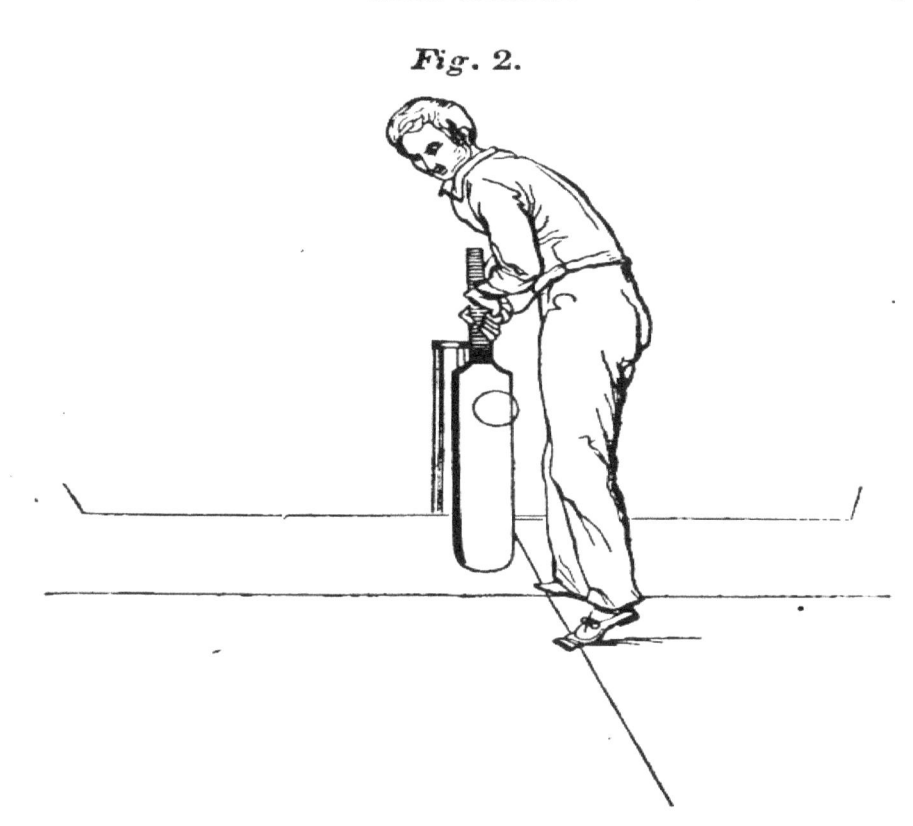

*Fig.* 2.

about the two leg stumps: for if you begin, as in *fig.* 1., with point of bat thrown back true to middle stump, you cannot bring the bat straight to meet a leg stump ball without the line of the bat and the line of the ball forming an angle in crossing each other; and, by keeping your wrists well back, and giving a clear space between body and wicket, the Draw will follow of itself.

The bat must not be purposely presented edgeways in the least degree. Draw a full bat from the line of the middle stump to meet a leg-stump ball, and you will have the benefit of a hit without lessening your defence. " A Draw is very dangerous with a ball that would hit the leg-stump," some say; but only when attempted in the wrong way; for how can a full bat increase your danger?

This mode of play will also lead to, what is most valuable, but most rare, a correct habit of passing every ball the least on side of middle stump clear away to the on side. This blocking between legs and wickets first obviates the ball going off legs into wicket; secondly, it keeps many awkward balls out of Slip's hands; and, thirdly, it makes single runs off the best balls.

Too little, now-a days, is done with the Draw; too much is attempted by the "blind swipe," to the loss of many wickets.

Every man, in a first-rate match, who loses his wicket, while swiping round, ought to pay a forfeit to the Reward Fund.

The only balls for the Draw are those which threaten the wicket. To shuffle backwards half a yard, scraping the bat on the ground, or to let the ball pass one side the body, with a blind swing on the other, are hits which to mention is to reprove.

Our good friend, Mr. Abraham Bass,—and what

cricketer in the Midland Counties defers not to his judgment,—thinks that the Draw cannot be made quite so much of as we say, except by a left-handed man. The short-pitched balls, which some draw, he thinks, are best played back to middle On by a turn of the left arm to the On side.

Here Mr. Bass mentions a very good hit—a good variety—and one, too, little practised : his hit and the Draw are each good in their respective places. To discriminate every shade is impossible. " Mr. Taylor had most hits I ever saw," said Caldecourt, " and was a better player, even, than Lord Frederick ; though Mr. Taylor's hits were not all *legitimate :* " so much the better ; new combinations of old hits.

The old-fashioned hit under left leg, Mr. Mynn, at Leicester, in 1836, gave great effect to one variety of it ; a hit which Pilch makes useful, though hard to make elegantly. Some say, with Caldecourt, such balls ought always to be drawn ; but is it not a useful variety ?

DRAW OR GLANCE FROM OFF STUMP.—What is true of the Leg stump is true of the Off, care being taken of catch to slips. Every ball played from two off stumps by free play of wrist and left shoulder well over should go away among the Slips. Play hard on the ball ; the ball must never hit a dead bat ; and every so-called block, from off stumps, must be a hit.

Commence, as always, from *fig.* 1 ; stand close up to

your wicket; weight on pivot-foot; balance-foot ready to come over as required. This is the only position from which you can command the off-stump.

Bear with me, my friends, in dwelling so much on this Off-play. Many fine cutters could never in their lives command off-stump with a full and upright bat. Whence come the many misses of off-hits? Observe, and you will see it is because the bat is slanting, or it must sweep the whole space through which the ball could rise.

By standing close up, and playing well over your wicket with straight bat, and throwing, by means of left leg, the body forwards, over a ball rising to the off-stump, you may make an effective hit from an off-bailer without lessening your defence; for how can hard blocking, with a full bat, be dangerous? All that is required, is, straight play and a free wrist, though certainly a tall man has here a great advantage.

A FREE WRIST.—Without wrist-play, there can be no good style of batting. Do not be puzzled about "throwing your body into your hit." Absurd, except with straight hits—a volley, for instance. Suspend a ball, oscillating by a string from a beam, keep your right foot fixed, and use the left leg to give the time and command of the ball, and adjust the balance, and you will soon learn the power of the wrists and arms. Also, use no heavy bats; 2 lbs. 2 oz. is heavy enough for any man who plays with his wrists. The wrist has, anatomically, two movements; the one up and down, the other from side to side; and to the latter power, by much the least, the weight of the bat must be proportioned. "My old-fashioned bat," said Mr. E. H. Budd, "weighed nearly three pounds, and Mr. Ward's a pound more."

THE OFF-HIT, here intended, is made with upright bat, where the horizontal cut were dangerous or uncertain. It may be made with any off-ball, one or two feet wide of the wicket. The left shoulder must be well over the ball, and this can only be effected by crossing, as in *fig.* 3, p. 147, left leg over. This, one of the best players agrees, is a correct hit, provided the ball be pitched well up; otherwise he would apply the Cut. But the cut serves only when a ball rises; and I am unwilling to spare one that comes in near the ground.

This upright off-hit, with left leg crossed over, may be practised with a bat and ball in the path of a field. You may also devise some "Chamber Practice," without any ball, or a soft ball suspended: not a bad indoor exercise in cold weather. When proficient, you will find that you have only to hit at the ball, and the balance-foot will naturally cross over and adjust itself.

In practising with a bowler I have often fixed a fourth stump, about six inches from off-stump, and learnt to guard it with upright bat. *Crede experto,* you may learn to sweep with almost an upright bat balls as much as two feet to the off. But this is a hit for balls requiring back play, but

COVER-HIT is the hit for over-pitched off-balls. Come forward hard to meet an off-ball, and then as your bat moves in one line, and the ball meets it in another, the resultant will be Cover-hit. By no means turn the bat: a full face is not only safe, but effective.

With all off-hits beware of the bias of the ball to the off, and play well over the ball—very difficult for young players. Never think about what off-hits you can make, unless you keep the ball safely down.

The fine square leg-hit is similar to cover-hit, though on the other side. To make cover-hit clean, and not waste power against the ground, you must take full advantage of your height, and play the bat well down on the ball from your hip, timing nicely, eye still on the ball, and inclining the bat neither too little nor too much.

THE FORWARD CUT, a name by which I would distinguish another off-hit, is a hit made by Butler, Guy, Dakin, Parr, and especially by the Nottingham men, who, Clarke thinks, "hit all round them" better than men of any other county (see *fig.* 3). Though the figures being foreshortened as seen by the bowler, the artist unwillingly sacrifices effect to show the correct position of the feet. This hit may be made from balls too wide and too low for the backward cut. Cross the left leg over, watch the ball from its pitch,

FORWARD CUT. 147

*Fig. 3.*

and you may make off hits from balls low or cut balls high (unless very high, and then you have time to drop the bat) with more commanding power than in any other position. Caldecourt does not like this crossing of left foot; but I know, from experience and observation, that there is not a finer or more useful hit in the field; though let me here attest that Caldecourt is admitted to be one of the best of instructors; and, " in my day," said Mr. E. H. Budd, " one of the best fieldsmen in England."

The forward cut is peculiar in this, that, if a ball is

some two feet to the off, it matters not whether overpitched or short-pitched, the same position, rather forward, equally applies.

This hit sends the ball between point and middle wicket a good part of the field, and even to long-field sometimes: no little advantage. Also, it admits of much greater quickness.

Fix a fourth stump in the ground, one foot or more wide to the off; practise carefully, keeping right foot fixed, and crossing left over, and preserve the cutting attitude; and this most brilliant hit is easily acquired.

When you play a ball off, do not lose your balance and stumble awkwardly one foot over the other, but end in good form, well on your feet. Even good players commit this fault; also in playing back they look as if they would tumble over their wicket.

THE CUT is generally considered the most delightful hit in the game. The cut proper is made by very few. Many make off-hits, but few " cut from the bails between short slip and point with a late horizontal bat, cutting, never by guess but always by sight, at the ball itself; the cut applying to rather short-pitched balls, not actually long hops; and that not being properly a cut which is in advance of the point." Such is the definition of Mr. Bradshaw, whom ten years' retirement has not prevented from being known as one of the best hitters of the day.

The attitude of cutting is faintly given (because fore-

THE CUT.—NO. 1. 149

*Fig.* 4.

shortened) in *fig.* 4. This represents a cut at rather a wide ball; and a comparison of *figs.* 3 and 4, will show that, with rather wide off balls, the forward cut is the better position; for you more easily intercept balls before they are out of play. Right leg would be rather thrown back than advanced were the ball nearer the wicket. Still the attitude is exceptional. Look at the other figures, and the cut alone will appear with right foot shifted. Compare *fig.* 1, with the other figures, and the change is easy, as in the left foot alone;

13*

but compare it with the cuts (*figs.* 4 and 5,) and the whole position is reversed: right shoulder advanced, and right foot shifted. There is no ball that can be cut which may not be hit by one of the other off hits already mentioned, and that with far greater certainty, though not with so brilliant an effect. Pilch and many of the steadiest and best players never make the genuine cut. "Mr. Felix," says Clarke, "cuts splendidly; but, in order to do so, he cuts before he sees the ball, and thus misses two out of three." Neither do I believe that any man will reconcile the habitual straight play and command of off-stump that distinguishes Pilch with a cutting game. Each virtue, even in cricket, has its excess: fine leg hitters are apt to endanger the leg-stump; fine cutters, the off. For the cutter must begin to take up his altered position so soon, that the idea must be running in his head almost while the ball is being delivered; then the first efforts bring the bat at once out of all defensive and straight play. Right shoulder involuntarily starts forward; and if at the wrong kind of ball, the wicket is exposed, and all defence at an end. But with long hops there is time enough to cut: the difficulty is with good balls, and to cut them, not by guess but by sight. *Fig.* 4 represents a cut at a ball nearer the wicket, the right foot being drawn back to gain space.

So much for the abuse of cutting. If the ball does not rise, there can be no cut, however loose the bowl-

THE CUT.—NO. 2.          151

*Fig.* 5.

ing; though, with the other off-hits, two or three might be scored. The most winning game is that which plays the greatest number of balls—an art in which no man can surpass Mr. Baldwinson. Still a first-rate player should have a command of every hit: a bowler may be pitching regularly short, and the balls may be regularly rising: in this case every one would, like to see a good cutter at the wicket.

To learn the cut, suspend a ball from a string and a beam, oscillating backwards and forwards—place yourself as at a wicket, and experimentalize. You will find:—

1. You have no power in cutting, unless you cut late—" off the bails : " then only can you use the point of your bat.

2. You have no power, unless you turn on the basis of your feet, and front the ball, your back being almost turned upon the bowler at the moment of cutting.

3. Your muscles have little power in cutting quite horizontally, but great power in cutting down on the ball.

This agrees with the practice of the best players. Mr. Bradshaw follows the ball and cuts very late, cutting down. He drops his bat apparently on the top of the ball. Lord Frederick used to describe the old-fashioned cutting as done in the same way. Mr. Bradshaw never cuts but by sight; and since, when the eye catches the rise of a good length ball, not a moment must be lost, his bat is thrown back just a little—an inch or two higher than the bails (he stoops a little for the purpose)—and dropped on the ball in an instant, by play of the wrist alone. Thus does he obtain his peculiar power of cutting by sight even fair-length balls.

Harry Walker, Robinson, and Saunders were the

three great cutters; and they all cut very late. But the under-hand bowling suited cutting (proper) better than round-armed; for all off-hitting is not cutting. Mr. Felix gives wonderful speed to the ball, effected by cutting down, adding the weight of a descending bat to the free and full power of the shoulder: he would hardly have time for such exertion if he hit with the precision of Mr. Bradshaw, and not hitting till he saw the ball.

Lord Frederick found fault with Mr. Felix's picture of "the cut," saying it implied force from the whirl of the bat; whereas a cut should proceed from wrists alone, descending with bat in hand,—precisely Mr. Bradshaw's hit. "Excuse me, my Lord," said Mr. Felix, "that's not a cut, but only a *pat*." The said *pat*, or wrist play, I believe to be the only kind of cutting by sight for good-length balls.

To encourage elegant play, and every variety of hit, we say practise each kind of cut, both Lord Frederick's *pat* and Mr. Felix's off-hit, and the Nottingham forward cut, with left leg over; but beware of using either in the wrong place. A man of one hit is easily managed. A good off-hitter should send the ball according to its pitch, not to one point only, but to three or four. Old Fennex used to stand by Saunders, and say no hitting could be finer—" no hitter such a fool— see, sir, they have found out his hit—put a man to stop his runs — still cutting, nothing but cutting —why does n't the man hit somewhere else?" So with Jarvis of Nottingham, a fine player and one of the best cutters of his day. When a man was placed for his cut, it greatly diminished his score. For off-balls we have given Off-play to the slips—Cover hit—the Nottingham hit more towards middle wicket; and the Cut between slip and point—four varieties. Let each have its proper place, till an old player can say, as Fennex said of Beldham, "He hit quick as lightning all round him. He appeared to have no hit in particular: you could never place a man against him: where the ball was pitched, there it was hit away."

LEG-HITTING.—Besides the draw, there are two distinct kinds of leg-hits—one forward, the other back. The forward leg-hit is made, as in *fig.* 6, by advancing the left foot near the pitch of the ball, and then hitting down upon the ball with a free arm, the bat being more or less horizontal, according to the length of the ball. A ball so far pitched as to require little stride of left leg will be hit with nearly a straight bat: a ball as short as you can stride to will require nearly a horizontal bat. The ball you can reach with straight bat will go off on the principle of the cover-hit—the more square the better. But when a ball is only just within reach, by using a horizontal bat, you know where to find the ball just before it has risen; for, your bat covers the space about the pitch. If you reach far enough, even a shooter may be picked up; and if a

LEG-HITTING. 155

**Fig. 6.**

few inches short of the pitch, you may have all the joyous spring of a half volley. The better pitched the bowling, the easier is the hit, if the ball be only a little to the leg. In using a horizontal bat, if you cannot reach nearer than about a foot from the pitch, sweep your bat through the line in which the ball should rise. Look at *fig.* 7, p. 160. The bat should coincide with or sweep a fair bat's length of the dotted line. But if point of bat cannot reach to within a foot of the pitch, that ball must be played back.

THE SHORT-PITCHED LEG BALL needs no comment, save that, according as it is more or less to the wicket, you may,—1. Draw it; 2. Play it by a new hit, to be explained, a Draw or glance outside your leg; 3. You may step back on your wicket to gain space, and play it away to middle On, or cut it round, according to your sight of it.

But in leg-hitting, beware of a "blind swipe," or that chance hit by guess of where the ball will rise, made when the bat cannot properly be played at the pitch. This blind hit is often made at a ball not short enough to play by sight back, nor long enough to command forward. Parr advances left foot as far as he can, and hits where the ball ought to be. But this he would hardly advise except you can nearly command the pitch; otherwise a blind swing of the bat, though you sometimes see it even among good players, is not to be recommended.

Reader, do you ever make this square hit On? Or do you ever drive a ball back from the leg-stump to long-field On? Probably not. Clarke complains that this good old hit is gone out, and one more man thereby brought about the wicket; and, if you cannot make this hit, you have a faulty style of playing leg-balls. So, practise diligently with leg-balls, till balls from two leg-stumps go to long-field On, and balls a little wide of leg-stump go nearly square; and do not do this by a kind of push—much too common,—but by a real hit, left shoulder forward.

Also, do you ever draw out of your ground to a leg-ball? Doubly dangerous is this—danger of stumping and danger of missing easy hits. If once you move your pivot foot, you lose that self-command essential for leg-hits. So, practise in your garden or your room the stride and swing of the bat, till you have learnt to keep your balance.

One of the best leg-hitters is Dakin, and his rule is: keep your right foot firm on your ground; advance the left straight to the pitch, and as far as you can reach, and hit as straight at the pitch as you can, just as if you were hitting to long-field: the ball will fly round square of itself.

My belief is, the Wykehamists introduced the art of hitting leg-balls at the pitch. When, in 1833, at Oxford, Messrs. F. B. Wright and Payne scored above sixty each off Lillywhite and Broadbridge, it was remarked by the players, they had never seen their leg-hit before. Clarke says he showed how to make forward leg-hits at Nottingham. For the Nottingham men used to hit after leg-balls, and miss them, till he found the way of intercepting them at the rise, and hitting square.

And this will be a fair occasion for qualifying certain

remarks which would appear to form what is aptly called a "toe-in-the-hole" player.

When I spoke so strongly about using the right foot as a pivot, and the left as a balance foot, insisting, also, on not moving the right foot, I addressed myself not to proficients, but to learners. Such is the right position for almost all the hits on the ball, and this fixing of the foot is the only way to keep a learner in his proper form.

Experienced players—I mean those who have passed through the University Clubs, and aspired to be chosen in the Gentlemen's Eleven of All England—must be able to move each foot on its proper occasion, especially with slow bowling. Clarke says, "If I see a man fast on his legs, I know he can't play my bowling." The reason is, as we shall explain presently, that the accurate hitting necessary for slow bowling requires, not long reaching, but a short, quick action of the arms and wrists, and activity on the legs, to shift the body to suit this hitting in narrow compass.

A practised player should also be able to go in to over-pitched balls to give effect to his forward play. To be stumped out looks ill indeed; still, a first-rate player should have confidence and coolness enough to bide his time, and then go boldly and steadily in and hit away. If you do go in, take care you go in far enough, and to the pitch, and only go in to straight balls, for to those alone can you carry a full bat. And never go in to make a free swing of the bat or tremendous swipe. Go in with a straight bat, not so much to hit as to drive or block the ball hard away, or, as Clarke says, "to run the ball down." Stepping in only succeeds with cool and judicious hitters, with some power of execution. All young players must be warned that for any but a most practised player to leave his ground is decidedly a losing game.

Supposing the batsman knows how to move his right foot back readily, the long-hop to the leg admits of various modes of play, which I feel bound to mention, though not to recommend; for a first-rate player should at least know every hit: whether he will introduce it much or little into his game is another question.

A leg-ball that can be played by sight is sometimes played by raising the left leg. This is quite a hit of the old school,—of Sparkes and Fennex, for instance. Fennex's pupil, Fuller Pilch, makes the hit commonly. Some first-rate judges—Caldecourt among others—maintain it should never be made, but the Draw always used instead. Mr. Taylor found it a useful variety; for, before he used it, Wenman used to stump him from balls inside leg stump. For some lengths it has certainly the advantage of placing the ball in a more open part of the field.

Another way to play such balls is to step back with the right foot, and thus gain time and length of hop, and play the ball away with short action of arm and

160   THE CRICKET FIELD.

*Fig.* 7.

wrist about middle On. This also is good, as making one hit more in your game. Another hit there is which bears a name not very complimentary to two, in many respects, excellent players, Marsden and Dean. Though Mr. Sampson, of Sheffield, say his friends, attains in a similar manner remarkable certainty in meeting legballs. My attention was first called to this hit by watching the play of Mr. E. Reeves, who makes it with all the ease and elegance of the Draw, of which I consider it one variety. Clarke says, that with a ball scarcely wide of your leg, he thinks it a good hit: I have, therefore, given a drawing of it in the last page. When done correctly, and in its proper place, it is made by an easy and elegant movement of the wrists, and looks as pretty as the Draw; but let me enter my protest against the absurd and useless distortions too commonly enacted by those who, carrying every novelty into excess, vainly endeavor to apply this hit to balls two or three feet wide. It is properly like the Draw, only it is made before the left leg instead of between right leg and wicket. It applies to a ball just too wide to draw conveniently; and I should be sorry to be held answerable for the abuse of this or any hit.

## CHAP. VIII.

### HINTS AGAINST SLOW BOWLING.

WHILE our ideas on Slow Bowling were yet in a state of solution, they were, all at once, precipitated and crystallized into natural order by the following remarks from a valued correspondent :—

" I have said that Pilch was unequalled with the bat, and his great excellence is in *timing* the ball. No one ever mastered Lillywhite like Pilch; because in his forward play he was not very easily deceived by that wary individual's repeated change of pace. He plays forward with his eye, not only on the pitch, but at the ball itself, being faster or slower in his advance by a calm calculation of time—a point too little considered by some even of the best batsmen of the day. No man hits much harder than Pilch; and, be it observed, hard hitting is doubly hard in all fair comparison when combined with that steady posture which does not sacrifice the defence of the wicket for some one favorite cut or leg-hit. Compare Pilch with good general hitters who, at the same time, guard their wicket, and I doubt if you can find from this select class a harder hitter in England."

"But it is of slow bowling I am speaking, and Fuller is one of the few who play Old Clarke as he should be played; playing him back all day if he bowls short, and hitting him hard along the ground whenever he overpitches; and sometimes he will go in to Clarke's bowling, but not to make a furious swipe, but to 'run him down' with a straight bat. This going in to Clarke's bowling some persons think necessary for every ball, forgetting that 'discretion is the better part of' cricket; the consequence is that many wickets fall from positive long hops. Almost every man who begins to play against Clarke appears to think he is in honor bound to hit every ball out of the field, and every one who attempts it comes out, saying, 'What rubbish!— no play in it!' The truth being that there is a great deal of play in it, for it requires real knowledge of the game. You have curved lines to deal with instead of straight ones. 'But what difference does that make?' 'Why, all the difference.'

"The amusing part is, that this cry of 'What rubbish!' has been going on for years, and still the same error prevails."

Experience is not like anything hereditary: as the generations of eels do not get used to being skinned, so the generations of men do not get tired of doing the same foolish thing. Each must suffer *propriâ personâ*, and not by proxy. So the gradual development of the human mind against Clarke's bowling is for the most part this:—first, a state of confidence in hitting every ball; secondly, a state of disgust and contempt at what seems only too easy for a scientific player to practise; and, lastly, a slowly increasing conviction that the batsman must have as much head as the bowler, with patience to play an unusual number of good lengths.

Slow bowling is most effective when there is a fast bowler at the other end. It is very puzzling to alter your time in forward play from fast to slow, and slow to fast, every Over: so Clarke and Wisden work well together. A shooter from a slow bowler is sometimes found even more difficult than one from a fast bowler, and this for two reasons; first, the batsman is made up for slow time, and less prepared for fast; and, secondly, a slow ball admits of being pitched further up, and, therefore, if the fast shooter has more pace, the slow has the shorter distance to shoot into the wicket.

Compare the several styles of bowling in the following diagram. A good length ball, you see, pitches nearer to the bat in proportion to the slowness of its pace. Wisden is not so fast, nor is Clarke as slow, practically, as they respectively appear. With Wisden's straight lines it is far easier to calculate where the ball will pitch than with the curved lines and dropping balls of Clarke; and when Wisden's ball has pitched, though its pace is quicker, the distance it has

Slow Ball balls—Clarke's.

Fast Ball balls—Wisden's.

Medium pace—Lillywhite's.

Slow Shooters—Clarke's.

Medium pace Shooters—Lillywhite's.

Fast Shooters—Wisden's.

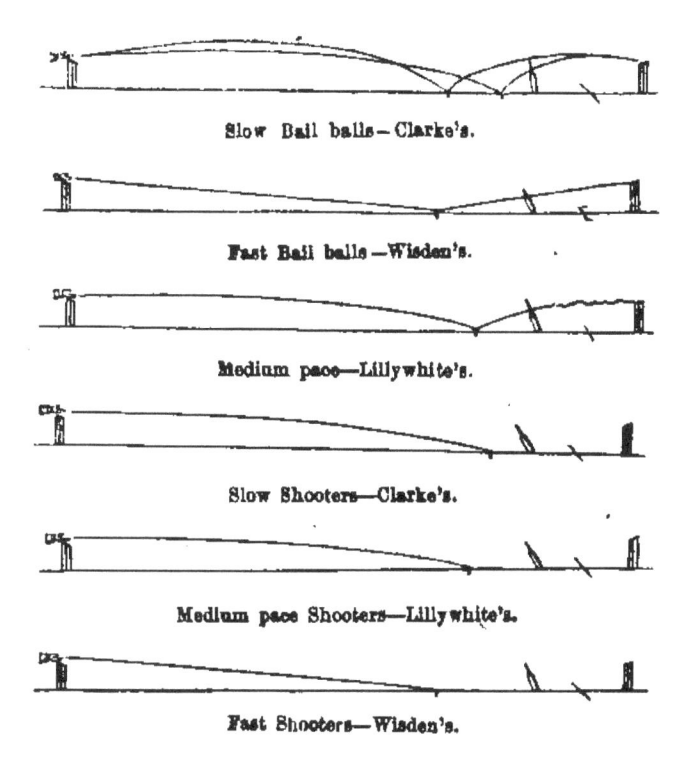

to come is so much longer, that Clarke, in effect, is not so much slower, as he may appear. Lillywhite and Hillyer are of a medium kind; having partly the quickness of Wisden's pace, and partly the advantage of Clarke's curved lines and far pitch. From this diagram it appears that the slower the bowling the nearer it may be pitched up, and the less is the space the bat can cover forward; also the more difficult is the ball to judge; for the curved line of a dropping ball is very deceiving to the eye.

In speaking of Clarke's bowling, men commonly imply that the slowness is its only difficulty. Now a ball cannot be more difficult for hand or eye because it moves slowly. No; the slower the easier; but the difficulty arises from the following qualities, wholly distinct from the slow pace, though certainly it is the slowness that renders these qualities possible:—

1st. Clarke's lengths are more accurate.

2dly. He can vary his pace unobserved, without varying his action or delivery.

3dly. More of his balls would hit the wicket.

4thly. A slow ball must be played: it will not play itself.

5thly. Clarke can more readily take advantage of each man's weak point.

6thly. Slow bowling admits of more bias.

7thly. The length is more difficult to judge, owing to the curved lines.

8thly. It requires the greatest accuracy in hitting. You must play at the ball with short, quick action where it actually is, and not by calculation of its rise, or where it will be.

9thly. Slow balls can be pitched nearer to the bat, affording a shorter sight of the rise.

10thly. Catches and chances of stumping are more frequent, and less likely to be missed.

11thly. The curved lines and the straightness preclude cutting, and render it dangerous to cross the ball in playing to leg.

One artifice of Clarke, and of all good slow bowlers, is this : to begin with a ball or two which may easily be played back ; then, with a much higher toss and slower pace, as in the diagram, he pitches a little short of the usual spot. If the batsman's eye is deceived as to the distance, he at once plays forward to a length which is at all times dangerous ; and, as it rises higher, it makes the play more dangerous still.

The difficulty of " going in " to such bowling as Clarke's, depends on this :

The bat is only four inches and a quarter wide : call half that width two inches of wood. Then you can only have two inches to spare for the deviation of your hit ; therefore, if a ball turns about two inches while you are in the act of hitting, the truest hitter possible must miss.

The obvious conclusion from these facts is :

1st. That you can safely go in to such balls only as are straight, otherwise you cannot present a full bat; and, only when you can step right up to the pitch of the ball, otherwise, by a twist, it will escape you; and slow balls twist more than fast. 2ndly. You can only go in to such lengths as you can easily and steadily command ; a very long step, or any unusual hurry, will hardly be safe with only the said two inches of wood to spare.

Now the question is, with what lengths, with such bowling as Clarke's, can you steadily and safely step in, as far as the pitch, with full command of hand and eye? Remember you cannot begin your step till you can judge the length; and this, with the curved line of a slow dropping ball, you cannot judge till within a little of its grounding; so the critical time for decision and action is very brief, and, in that brief space, how far can you step secure of all optical illusions, for Clarke can deceive you by varying both the pace and the curve of his ball?—Go and try. Again, when you have stepped in, where will you hit? On the ground, of course, and straight. And where are the men placed? Besides, are you aware of the difficulty of interchanging the steady game with right foot in your ground, with that springy and spasmodic impulse that characterizes this "going in?" At a match at Lord's, in 1849, I saw Brockwell score some forty runs with many hits off Clarke: he said to me, when he came out, "Clarke cannot bowl his best to me; for sometimes I go in to the pitch of the ball when pitched well up, and hit her away; at other times, I make a feint, and then stand back, and so Clarke gets off his bowling." He added, "the difficulty is to keep your temper, and not to go in with a wrong ball." This, I believe, is indeed a difficulty,—a much greater difficulty than is commonly imagined. My advice to all players who have not made a study of the art of going in, and have not fully succeeded on practising days, is by no means to attempt it in a match. It is not so easy as it appears. You will find Clarke, or any good slow bowler, too much for you. "But supposing I should stand out of my ground, or start before the ball is out of the bowler's hand?" Why, with an unpractised bowler, especially if in the constrained attitude of the overhand delivery, this manœuvre has succeeded in producing threes and fours in rapid succession. But Clarke would pitch over your head, or send in a quick underhand ball a little wide, and you would be stumped; and Wisden would probably send a fast toss about the height of your shoulder. and, being prepared to play perfectly straight at the pitch, you would hardly raise your bat in time to keep a swift toss out of the wicket-keeper's hands.

The difficulty of curvilinear bowling is this:

1st. In making a catch every fieldsman finds that, in proportion as the ball has been hit up in the air, it is difficult to judge where to place himself. By the same law of sight, a fast ball that goes almost point-blank to its pitch, is far easier to judge than a slow ball that descends in a curve.

2dly. As the slow ball reaches the ground at a greater angle, it must rise higher in a given space; so, if the batsman misjudges the pitch of a slow ball by a foot, he will misjudge the rise to a greater extent than with a fast ball that rises less abruptly. Hence, playing forward is less easy with slow than with fast bowling.

3dly. As to timing the ball, all the eye can discern

in a body moving directly towards it, is the angle with the ground: to see the curve of a dropping ball you must have a side view. The man at Point can see the curve clearly; but not so the batsman. Consequently, the effect of the curve is left out in the calculation, and the exact time of the ball's approach is, to that extent, mistaken. Every one knows the difficulty of making a good half-volley hit off a slow ball, because the timing is so difficult: great speed without a curve is less puzzling to the eye than a curvilinear movement, however slow. It were odd, indeed, if it were harder to hit a slow than a fast ball. No. It is the curve that makes difficult what of its pace alone would be easy. All forward play with slow bowling is beset with the same difficulty of allowing for the curve. And what style of play does this suggest? Why, precisely what Clarke has himself remarked,— namely, that to fix the right foot as for fast bowling, and play with long reach forward, does not answer. You must be quick on your feet, and, by short, quick action of the arms, hit the ball actually as it is, and not as you calculate it will be a second later. This is the system of men who play Clarke best; of Pilch, of Dakin, of Hunt of Sheffield, and of C. Browne: though these men also dodge Clarke; and, pretending sometimes to go out, deceive him into dropping short, and so play their heads against his. The best bowling is sometimes hit; but I have not heard of any man who found it much easier to score off Clarke than off other good bowlers.

Again, as to cutting, or in any way crossing, these dropping or curvilinear balls. As a slow ball rises twice as much in a given space as a fast ball, of course the chances are greater that the bat will not cover the ball at the point at which, by anticipation, you cut. If you cut at a fast ball, the height of its rise is nearly uniform, and its course a straight line : so most men like very fast bowling, because, if the hand is quick enough, the judgment is not easily deceived, for the ball moves nearly in straight lines. But, in cutting or in crossing a slow ball, the height varies enough to produce a mistake before the bat can meet it.

Once more, in playing at a ball after its rise, a safe and forcible hit can only be made in two ways. You must either meet the ball with full and straight bat, or cut horizontally across it. Now, as slow balls generally rise too high for a hard hit with perpendicular bat, you are reduced generally to the difficulties of cutting or back play. Add to all this that the bias from the hand and from the inequalities of the ground is much greater, and also that a catch remains commonly so long in the air that every fieldsman can cover double his usual quantity of ground, and then we shall cease to wonder that the best players cannot score fast off slow bowling.

## CHAP. IX.

BOWLING.—AN HOUR WITH "OLD CLARKE."

In cricket wisdom Clarke is truly " Old : " what he has learnt from anybody, he learnt from Lambert. But he is a man who thinks for himself, and knows men and manners. " I beg your pardon, sir," he one day said to a gentleman taking guard, " but ain't you Harrow ? " —" Then we shan't want a man down there," he said, addressing a fieldsman; " stand for the ' Harrow drive,' between point and middle wicket."

The time to see Clarke is the morning of a match. While others are practising, he walks round, with his hands under the flaps of his coat, reconnoitering his adversaries' wicket.

" Before you bowl to a man, it is worth something to know what is running in his head. That gentleman," he will say, " is too fast on his feet, so, as good as ready money to me : if he does n't hit he can't score ; if he does, I shall have him."

Going a little further, he sees a man lobbing to another, who is practising stepping in. " There, sir, is 'practising to play Clarke,' that is very plain; and a nice mess, you will see, he will make of it. Ah! my friend, if you do go in at all, you must go in further than that, or my twist will beat you; and going in to swipe round, eh! Learn to run me down with a straight bat, and I will say something to you. But that would n't score quite fast enough for your notions. Going in to hit round is a tempting of Providence."

"There, that man is pure stupid: alter the pace and height with a dropping ball, and I shall have no trouble with him. They think, sir, it is nothing but 'Clarke's vexatious pace:' they know nothing about the curves. With fast bowling, you cannot have half my variety; and when you have found out the weak point, where 's the fast bowler that can give the exact ball to hit it? There is often no more head-work in fast bowling than there is in the catapult: without head-work, I should be hit out of the field."

"A man is never more taken aback than when he prepares for one ball, and I bowl him the contrary one: there was Mr. Nameless, the first time he came to Nottingham, full of fancies about playing me. The first ball he walked some yards out to meet me, and I pitched over his head, so near his wicket, that, thought I, that bird won't fight again. Next ball he was a little cunning, and made a feint of coming out, meaning, as I guessed, to stand back for a long hop; so I pitched right up to him; and he was so bent upon cutting me away, that he hit his own wicket down!"

Look at diagrams page 165. Clarke is there represented as bowling two balls of different lengths; but the increased height of the shorter pitched ball, by a natural ocular delusion, makes it appear as far pitched as the other. If the batsman is deceived in playing at both balls by the same forward play, he endangers his wicket. "See, there," continues Clarke, "that gentleman's *is* a dodge, certainly, but not a new one, either. He does step in, it is true; but, while hitting at the ball, he is so anxious about getting back again, that his position has all the danger of stepping in, and none of its advantages."

"Then there is Mr.———," naming a *great* man struggling with adversity. "He gives a jump up off his feet, and thinks he is stepping in, but comes flump down just where he was before."

"Pilch plays me better than any one. But he knows better than to step in to every ball, or to stand fast every ball. He plays steadily, and discriminates, waiting till I give him a chance, and then makes the most of it."

Bowling consists of two parts: there is the mechanical part, and the intellectual part. First, you want the hand to pitch where you please, and then the head to know where to pitch, according to the player.

The first thing is to gain full command over the ball; therefore,

1. Practise bowling quite within your strength. If your strength and stature is little, your pace cannot be fast. Be contented with being rather a slow bowler. By commencing slowly, if any pace is in you, it will not be lost; but, by commencing fast, you will spoil all.

2. Practise, says Lillywhite, "both sides of the wicket. To change sides is highly useful when the ground is worn, and it often proves puzzling to the batsman."

3. Hold the ball in the fingers, not in the palm. If the tips of the fingers touch the seam of the ball, some bowlers find it assists in the spin.

4. The essence of a good delivery is sending the ball forth rotating, or turning on its own axis. The more spin you give the ball, the better the delivery; because then the ball will twist, rise quickly, or cut variously, the instant it touches the ground.

5. This spin must not proceed from any conscious action of the fingers, but from some mechanical action of the arm and wrist. Clarke is not conscious of any attempt to make his ball spin or twist: a certain action has become habitual to him. He may endeavor to increase this tendency sometimes; but no bowling could be uniform that depended so much on the nerves, or on such nice feeling as this attention to the fingers would involve. A bowler must acquire a certain mechanical

swing, with measured steps and uniform action and carriage of the body. Still, at length, as with shooting, hand and eye naturally go together. In rowing, if you look at your oar, you cut crabs. In skating, if you look at the ice and think of your steps, you lose the freedom and the flow of your circles. So, with bowling, you must, of course, try experiments till you have decided on your steps and one mode of delivery, and then practise no other, and think more of the wicket than of your feet or your hand.

6. Commence with a very low delivery. Cobbett, and others of the best bowlers, began underhand. The lower the hand, the more the spin, and the quicker the rise. Unfair or throwing bowlers never have a first-rate delivery. See how easy to play is a throw or a ball from a catapult; and simply because the ball has then no spin.

7. Practise a little and often. If you overfatigue the muscles, you spoil their tone for a time. Bowling, as we said of batting, must become a matter of habit; and habits are formed by frequent repetition. Let the bowlers of Eton, Harrow, and Winchester, resolve to bowl if it be but a dozen balls every day, wet or fine. Intermission is very prejudicial. Also, never practise carelessly: always do your best, and always in the same form, lest you create a contrary habit.

8. The difficulty is to pitch far enough. Commence, according to your strength, eighteen, or nineteen yards,

and increase to twenty-two by degrees. Most amateurs bowl long hops.

9. Seek accuracy more than speed: a man of fourteen stone is not to be imitated by a youth of eight stone. Many players like swift bowling, and why? Because the length is easier to judge; the lines are straighter for a cut; the ball wants little accuracy of hitting; fast bowlers very rarely pitch quite as far even as they might, for this requires much extra power; fast balls twist less, and rarely increase their speed so much at the rise; fast bowling gives fewer chances that the fieldsman can take advantage of, and admits generally of less variety; fewer fast balls are pitched straight, and fewer even of those would hit the wicket. You may find a Redgate, a Wisden, or a Mynn, who can bring fast bowling under command for one or two seasons; but they are exceptions so solitary as to make no precedent. Even these men were naturally of a fast pace: swiftness was not their chief object. So, study accurate bowling, and let speed come of itself. In speaking of an amateur, who took much kind interest in the play of one of the public schools, Clarke said he could not bear to see so many promising young players taught a wild style of bowling: it was nothing short of " cruelty to animals."

So much for attaining the power of a bowler; next to apply that power:

1. Pitch as near the bat as you can without being hit

away. The bowler's chance is to compel back play with the shortest possible sight of the rise.

2. If three good balls have been stopped, the fourth is often destructive, because the batsman's patience is exhausted: so .take pains with the fourth ball of the over.

3. The straighter the ball, the more puzzling to the eye, and the more cramping to the hand of the batsman.

4. Short-pitched balls are not only easier to hit, but have more scope for missing the wicket, though pitched straight.

5. A free leg-hitter may often be put out by placing an extra man On side, and bowling repeatedly at leg-stump—only do not pitch very far up to him. Short-pitched leg-balls are the most difficult to hit, and produce most catches. By four or five attempts at leg-hitting, a man gains a tendency to swing round, and is off his straight play.

6. Besides trying every variety of length, vary your pace to deceive the batsman in timing his play; and practise the same action so as not to betray the change of pace. Also, try once or twice a high dropping ball.

7. Learn to bowl tosses and tices. With a stiff player, before his eye is in, a toss often succeeds; but especially practise high lobs—a most useful variety of ball. In most Elevens there are one or two men with

whom good round-hand bowling is almost thrown away. A first-rate player in Warwickshire was found at fault with lobs: and till he learnt the secret, all his fine play was at an end.

8. Find out the furthest point to which your man can play forward safely, and pitch just beyond that point with every variety of pace and dropping balls.

9. A good under-hand ball of two high curves—that is, a dropping ball rising high—is produced thus :— Run fast to deliver the ball, and toss it six or seven feet in the air: when it touches the ground, it will rise and come in faster than expected, from the impetus derived from the run. Such a ball, with a twist into leg-stump, and a third man to On side, is very effective, producing both catch and stumping. This is well worth trying, with four men to the On side, if some great gun is brought to win a country match.

10. Most men have a length they cannot play. The fault of young bowlers is, they do not pitch far enough, and thus afford too long a sight of the ball. In the school matches and the university matches at Lord's, this is very observable, especially with fast bowlers.

11. The old fashioned underhand lobbing, if governed by a good head—dropping short when a man is coming out, and sometimes tossed higher and sometimes lower,— is a valuable change in most Elevens; but it must be high and accurately pitched, and must have head-work in it. Put long-stop upon the On

side, and bring long-slip nearer in; and be sure that your long-fields stand far away.

12. Lastly, the last diagram explains that curvilineal bowling, the effect of a moderate pace and a spin, gives the batsman a shorter sight of the rise than is possible with the straighter lines of swift bowling. A man has nearly as much time to make up his mind and prepare for Wisden as for Clarke, because he can judge Wisden's ball much sooner, and, though the rise is faster, it has further to come in.

THEORY OF BOWLING.—What characterizes a good delivery? If two men bowl with equal force and precision, why does the ball come in from the pitch so differently in respect of cutting, twisting, or abrupt rise?

"Because one man gives the ball so much more rotatory motion on its own axis, or so much more spin than the other."

A throw, or the catapult which strikes the ball from its rest, gives no spin; hence, the ball is regular in its rise, and easy to calculate.

Cobbett gave a ball as much spin as possible: his fingers appeared wrapped round the ball: his wrist became horizontal: his hand thrown back at the delivery, and his fingers seemingly unglued joint by joint, till the ball quitted the tips of them last, just as you would spin a top. Cobbett's delivery designed a sp'n, and the ball at the pitch had new life in it. No bowling so fair, and with so little rough play or violence, ever proved more effective than Cobbett's. Hillyer is entitled to the same kind of praise.

A spin is given by the fingers; also by turning the hand over in delivering the ball.

A good ball has two motions — one straight, from hand to pitch, the other on its own axis.

The effect of a spin on its own axis is best exemplified by bowling a child's hoop. Throw it from you without any spin, and away it rolls; but spin or revolve it against the line of its flight with great power, and the hoop no sooner touches the ground than it comes back to you. So great a degree of spin as this cannot possibly be given to a cricket ball; but you see the same effect in the " draw-back stroke " at billiards. Revolve the hoop with less power, and it will rise abruptly from the ground and then continue its course — similar to that awkward and abrupt rise often seen in the bowling of Clarke among others.

Thirdly, revolve the hoop as you bowl it, not *against* but *in* the line of its flight, and you will have its tendency to bound expended in an increased quickness forward. This exemplifies a low swimming ball, quickly cutting in and sometimes making a shooter. This is similar to the " following stroke " at billiards, made by striking the ball high and rotating it in the line of the stroke.

Such are the effects of a ball spinning or rotating vertically.

Now try the effect of a spin from right to left, or left to right: try a side stroke at billiards; the apparent angle of reflection is not equal to the angle of incidence. So a cricket ball, with lateral spin, will work from Leg to Off, or Off to Leg, according to the spin.

But why does not the same delivery, as it gives the same kind of spin, always produce the same vertical or lateral effect on a ball? In other words, how do you account for the fact that (apart from roughness of ground) the same delivery produces sometimes a contrary twist? "Because the ball may turn in the air, and the vertical spin become lateral. What was the under side may at the pitch be the upper, or the upper become under, or any modification of either may be produced in conjunction with inequality in the ground."

With throwing bowling the ball comes from the ends of the fingers; why, then, does it not spin? Because, unlike Cobbett's delivery, as explained, wherein the ball left the fingers by degrees, and was sent spinning forth, the ball, in a throw, is held between fingers and thumb, which leave their hold at the same instant, without any tendency to rotate the ball. The fairer and more horizontal the delivery the more the fingers act, the more spin, and the more variety, after the pitch. A high and unfair delivery, it is true, is difficult from the height of the rise; otherwise it is too regular and easy to calculate, to make first-rate bowling.

## CHAP. X.

#### HINTS ON FIELDING.

THE essence of good fielding is to start before the ball is hit, and to pick up and return straight to the top of the bails by one continuous action. This was the old Wykehamist style—old, I hope not yet extinct, past revival; — for, some twenty years since, the Wykehamist fielding was unrivalled by any school in England. Fifteen years ago, Mr. Ward and, severally and separately, Cobbett instanced a Winchester Eleven as the first fielding they had ever seen at Lord's. And among this chosen number were the yet remembered names of R. Price, F. B. Wright, Knatchbull, and Meyrick. These hardy Trojans—for the ball never came too fast for them—commenced fagging out long, very long, before they were indulged in batting, and were forced to qualify even for fagging, by practising till they could throw over a certain neighboring barn, and were always in bodily fear of the pains and penalties of the middle stump if ever they missed a ball. But these days of the voluntary system are far less favorable for fielding. To become a good fieldsman requires persevering practice, and a " big fellow " to fag for who will expect a little more smartness than is always developed by pure love of the game.

And now Etonians, Harrovians, Wykehamists, I mention you alphabetically, a few words on training your Eleven for Lord's. Choose first your bowlers and wicket-keeper and long-stop; these men you must have, though not worth a run: then, if you have any batsmen decidedly superior, you may choose them for their batting, though they happen not to be first-rate fieldsmen. But in most school Elevens, after naming four or five men, it is mere chance who scores among the other six or seven; so let any great superiority in fielding decide the choice. I remember playing a match in which I had difficulty in carrying the election of a first-rate fieldsman against a second-rate bat. Now the said batsman could not certainly be worth above fourteen runs; say seven more than the fieldsman. But the fieldsman, as it happened, made a most difficult catch, put one runner out, and, above all, kept the bowlers in good heart, during an up-hill game, by stopping many hard hits. A bad fieldsman is a loose screw in your machinery; giving confidence to the adversary, and taking the spirit out of his own party. Therefore, let the captain of an Eleven proclaim that men must qualify by fine fielding: and let him encourage the following exercises:

Put in two batsmen, whose play is not good enough

to spoil, to tip and run. You will find what very clean fielding is required to save one run with men determined to try it.

Let every man practise long-stop.

Let the wicket-keeper take his place, and while some one throws or hits, let him require the quickest and most accurate throwing. A ball quickly thrown comes in like a dart—no time being lost high in air. At short distances throw at once to the hands; at longer distances with a long hop. The hop should result from a low and skimming throw, or the ball will lose its speed. Practise throwing, without any flourish, by a single action of the arm. Any good fieldsman will explain, far better than our pen, the art of picking up a ball in the only position consistent with a quick return. A good throw often runs a man out; an advantage very rarely gained without something superior in fielding. Young players should practise throwing. The captain should keep an account of the best runners, throwers, clean pickers-up, and especially of men who can meet and anticipate the ball, and of those who deserve the praise given to Chatterton—" the safest pair of hands in England."

So much for quick throwing; but for a throw up from long field, Virgil had a good notion of picking up and sending in a ball:

"Ille manu raptum trepida torquebat in hostem;
Altior assurgens, et cursu concitus, heros."
*Æn.* xii. 901.

Here we have snatching up the ball with a quiver of the wrist, rising with the effort, and a quick step or two to gain power. Meeting the ball requires a practice of its own, and is a charming operation when you can do it: for the same impetus with which you run in assists the quickness of your return. Practice will reveal the secret of running in; only run with your hands near the ground, so as not to have suddenly to stoop; and keep your eyes well open, not losing the ball for an instant. In fielding, as in batting, you must study all the varieties of balls, whether tices, half volleys, or other lengths.

A fast runner *nascitur non fit:* still, practice does much, and especially for all the purposes of a fieldsman near the wicket. A spring and quick start are things to learn; and that both right and left: few men spring equally well with both feet. Anticipating the ball, and getting the momentum on the proper side, is everything in fielding; and practice will enable a man to get his proper footing, and quick shifting step. A good cricketer, like a good skater, must have free use of both feet, and of course a fine fieldsman must catch with both hands.

Practise left-handed catching in a ring; also picking up with left: "Any one can catch with his right," says the old player; " now, my boy, let us see what you can do with your left." Try, also, " slobbering " a ball, to see how many arts there are of recovering it afterwards. I need hardly say that jumping off your feet for a high catch, and rushing in to a ball and patting it up in the air and catching it the second attempt, are all arts of first-rate practitioners.

*Safe Hands.*—Your hands should be on the rat-trap principle,—taking anything in, and letting nothing out again. Of course a ball has a peculiar feeling and spin off a bat quite different from a throw; so practise accordingly. By habit hand and eye will go together: what the eye sees the right part of the hand will touch by a natural adjustment. There is a way of allowing for the spin of the ball in the air: as to its tendency at Cover, to twist especially to the left, this is too obvious to require notice.

I am ashamed to be obliged to remind players, old as well as young, that there is such a thing as being a good judge of a short run: and I might hold up, as an example, an *Honorable* gentleman, who, though a first-rate long stop and fine style of batting, has a distinct reputation for the one run. It is a tale, perhaps, thrice told, but more than thrice forgotten, that the partner should follow up the ball; how many batsmen destroy the very life of the game by standing still like an extra umpire! Now, in a school Eleven, running matches can be practised with security, because with mutual dependence; though I would warn good players that, among strangers in a country match, sharp running is a dangerous game. To lose single runs involves additional loss from the adversary standing where he pleases. I have heard of a gentleman for years accounted a good long stop, till some men were put in against him to try his powers,—Clarke, I think, was one,—and they hurried him so much that, from that hour, he abdicated.

Let old players keep up the habit of throwing and active movements. For the redundant spirit and buoyancy of youthful activity soon goes. Many a zealous cricketer loses his once famed quickness from mere disuse—*Sic omnia fatis, in pejus ruere.* Instead of always batting and practising poor Hillyer and Wisden till their dodges are dodges no more, and it is little credit to score from them, go to your neighbor's wicket and practise fielding for an hour, or else next match your throwing will be at fault.

Fielding, I fear, is retrograding: a good general player, famed for that quick return that runs the adversary out, and, at the same time, a useful change in bowling,—a judge of a run, and respectable at every point of the game: this is becoming a scarce character, and batting is a word supposed coextensive with cricket,—a sad mistake.

SPARE THE BOWLER.—One reason for returning the ball, not to bowler, but to wicket-keeper, he should advance quietly and return slowly a catch. A swift throw, or any exertion in the field that hurts the bowler's hand, or sets it shaking, may lose a game. If a bowler has half volleys returned to him, by stretching and stooping after them, he gets out of his swing. Now this same swing is a great point with a bowler. Watch him after he has got his footsteps firm for his feet, and when in his regular stride, and see the increased precision of his performance. Then comes the time when your great gun tumbles down his men: and that is the time that some sure judgmatic batsman, whose eminence is little seen amidst the loose hitting of a scratch match, comes calmly and, composedly to the wicket and makes a stand; and, as he disposes of maiden overs, and steals ones and twos, he breaks the spell that bound his men, and makes the dead-straight bowling good for cuts and leg hits. In no game or sport do I ever witness half the satisfaction of the bowler who can thus bowl maiden overs and defy a score; or of the batsman who takes the edge off the same, runs up the telegraph to even betting, and gives easier work and greater confidence to those who follow. A wicket-keeper, too, may dart off and save a bowler from fielding a three or four; and, whenever he leaves his wicket, slip must take wicket-keeper's place: how stale! true; but,—*instantly* 's the word,—from neglect of which, we have seen dreadful mistakes made even in good matches.

Ay, and what beautiful things are done by quick return and a low shy; no time wasted in parabolic curves: ball skimming the ground and coming in a long hop, but quickest of all returns (not safest) is a volley to the top of the bails into wicket-keeper's hands.

POINT.—Your great strength lies in anticipation: witness Ἄναξ ἀνδρῶν. To that gentleman every ball seems hit, because he always gets thereabouts; yet is he near-sighted withal! 'T is the mind that sees, eyes are its glasses, and he is too good a workman to want excuse for his tools. With slow bowling and bad batsman, Point can anticipate easily enough. Still, with all bowling, fast and slow, the common fault of point is, that he stands, if near, too near, and if far off, yet not far enough off. Stand where you yourself can catch and stop. If slow in hand and eye, stand off for longer catches, else, by standing where a quick man would catch sharp catches, you miss everything. With fast bowling, few balls that could be caught at seven yards ground short of twelve. Though, if the ground is very rough, or the bowling slow, the ball may be popped up near the bat, even by good players. Whenever a ball is hit off, point must cross *instanter*, or he'll be too late to back up, especially bowler's wicket.

Point is sometimes Point proper, like a wicket-keeper or shortslip, to cramp the batsman, and take advantage of his mistakes; but, with fast bowling and good batsmen, Point may advantageously stand off like any other fieldsman. For then he will save many more runs, and may make quite as many catches. If Mr.

King stood as Point, and Chatterton as cover in the same line, with Pilch batting and Wisden bowling, they would not (as I presume they are well aware) work to the best advantage. When Clarke is bowling to one of twenty-two, the case is different; he wants a veritable Point for the catch.

SHORTLEG is often a very hardly used personage, expected to save runs that seem easy, but are actual impossibilities. A good ball, perhaps, is pushed forward to middle wicket. On shortleg being square, then the bowler looks black at him. Then a draw is made, when shortleg is standing sharp in forward, and no man is ubiquitous. If the batsman often does not know where the rise or bias may reflect the ball, how should the fieldsman know?

COVERPOINT and LONGSLIP are both difficult places; the ball comes so fast and curling, that it puzzles even the best man. No place in the field but longstop has the work of longslip. This used to be Pilch's place.

The chief point in these places is to stand either to save one or to save two. This depends on the quickness of the fieldsman and the judgment of the runners. With such judges of a run as Hon. F. Ponsonby, Pilch, or Clarke, you must stand rather near to save one; but quick return is everything. Here Caldecourt was, years since, first-rate. I have seen him, when past his best, at Cover, judge well, start quick, run low, up and in like a shot to wicket-keeper's hands;

and what more would you have in fielding? When E. H. Budd played and won a second match for 100*l.* with Mr. Brande,—two fieldsmen given,—so much was thought of Mr. Brande's having engaged Caldecourt, that it was agreed he should field on both sides. He did so, and shied Mr. Budd out at a single stump. To save two, a good man may stand a very long way off on hard ground, and reduce the hardest cuts to singles. But a common fault is, "standing nowhere," neither to save one nor to save two. Remember not to stand as sharp when fast bowling is replaced by slow. Cover is the place for brilliant fielding. Watch well the batsman, and start in time. Half a spring in anticipation puts you already under weigh, and makes yards in the ground you can cover. The following is curious:

"You would think," said Caldecourt, "that a ball to the right hand may be returned more quickly than a ball to the left." But ask him, and he will show you how, if at a long reach, he always found it otherwise. The right shoulder may be even in the better position to return (in spite of change of hands) when the left picks up the ball than when the right picks it.

Some good Covers have been quicker with a hard jerk than a throw, for the attitude of fielding is less altered. Still, a jerk is less easy to the wicket-keeper. A longslip with good head and heels, may assist longstop; his triumph is to run a man out by anticipating the balls that bump off longstop's wrists and shins.

A third man up, or a middle slip, is at times very killing: this lets longslip stand back for hard hits, and no catch escapes. A forward point, or middle wicket close in, often snaps up a catch or two, particularly when the ground is dangerous for forward play, or the batsman plays hesitatingly.

Thick-soled shoes save colds in soppy weather, and do not jar when the ground is hard; for the Cantabs say that

$$\text{Thin soles} + \text{hard ground} = \text{tender feet,}$$

is an undeniable equation. Bowlers should wear worsted socks to save blisters, and mind the thread is not fastened off in a knot just under the most sensitive part of the heel.

Much inconvenience arises in a match, for the best player may be out by spectators standing in the eye of the ball; so stretch strips of white canvas on poles five feet high, for, while it keeps the stupid away, it provides a white back ground for each wicket.

This is good also in a park, where the deep shade of trees increases the confessed uncertainty of the game. Some such plan is much wanted on all public grounds where the sixpenny freeholders stand and hug their portly corporations in, and give the ball all the shades of green coat, light waistcoat, and drop-smalls, by standing in the line of the wicket. Still, batsmen must try to rise superior to such annoyances; for if the bowler changes his side of the wicket, the umpire often is in the light of the ball.

Oh! that ring at Lord's; for, as in olden time,—

―――― "si quid fricti ciceris probat et nucis emptor;"

that is, if the swillers of half-and-half and smokers of pigtail,—a preponderating influence and large majority of voices,—applaud a hit, it does not follow that it is a good one: nor, if they cry " Butterfingers!" need the miss be a bad one. No credit for good intentions!— no allowance for a twisting catch and the sun enough to singe your eyelids!—the hit that wins the "half-and-half" is the finest hit for that select assemblage, whose "sweet voices" quite drown the nicer judgment of the pavilion, even as vote by ballot would swamp the House of Lords.

LONGSTOP.—If you would estimate the value of a practised longstop, only try to play a match without one. Still, patient merit is rarely appreciated, for what is done very well looks so easy. Longstopping requires the cleanest handling and quickest return. The best in form I ever saw was an Oxonian about 1838,—a Mr. Napier. One of the worst in form, however, is the best of his day in practice,—Good; for he takes the ball sideways. A left-handed man, like Good, has a great advantage in stopping slips under-leg. Old Beagley, among the ancients, was the man. But there is many a man whose praise is yet unsung;

for when Mr. E. H. Budd saw Mr. R. Stodhert at Lansdown, Bath, stop right and left to Mr. Kirwan's bowling, he mentioned Beagley's doings, and said Beagley never came up to R. Stodhert. The gentleman who opposed the firmest front, however, for years to Messrs. Kirwan and Fellowes,—bowlers, who have broken studs into the breast-bone of a longstop, and then, to make amends, taken fourpenny-bits of skin off his shins,—is Mr. Hartopp, pronounced by Mr. Charles Burt,—himself undeniable at that point,—to be the best for a continuance he has ever seen. *Vigeat vireatque!* His form is good; works with great ease and cool attention. Among the most celebrated at present are Mr. C. Ridding, Nat. Pilch, and Guy.

One of the most practised longstops writes: " No place requires so much patient perseverance: the work is so mechanical. I have seen many a brilliant fieldsman there for a short innings while the bowling is straight and rarely passes; but let him have to humdrum through 150 or 200 runs, and they get bored, tired, and careless, and runs come apace. Patience is much wanted if a sharp runner is in, for he will often try a longstop's temper by stealing runs; then I have always found it the best plan to prepare the wicketkeeper for a hard throw to his, the nearer, wicket; for if you do not run the man out, you frighten him down to steadier running. Throwing over does sometimes answer; but a cunning runner will get in your way, or beat a ball thrown over his head. Longstop's distance must often be as much as four or five yards less for a good runner than a bad. Short distance does not make stopping more difficult because it gives fewer hops and twists to the ball; but a longer distance enables you to cover more tips and draws, and saves legbyes. Good runners ought to cross if the ball is in the least fumbled; but clean fielding, with quick underhand return, would beat the Regent Street Pet himself did he attempt it. Longstop is wholly at fault if he requires the wicket-keeper to favor him: this would spoil the stumping. As to gloves and pads, let every one please himself; he must choose between gloves and sore hands; but wrist gauntlets are of great use, and no hindrance to catches, which are usually spinning, and otherwise difficult.

As to form, dropping on one knee is a bad position for any fielding: you are fixed and left behind by any sudden turn of the ball. The best rule is to watch the ball from the bowler's hand and move accordingly, and you will soon find how much bias to allow; and beware of a slope like Lord's: it causes a greater deviation than you would imagine in thirty yards. Just as the ball comes, draw yourself up heels together (thus many a shooter have I stopped), and, picking as neatly as you can, pitch it back to wicket-keeper as if it were red hot. Quick return saves many byes, and keeps up an appearance which prevents the attempt. The same discrimination of lengths is required with hands as with bat. Long hops are easy: a tice is as hard almost as a shooter; half-volley is a teaser. Such balls as pitch up to you should be "played forward" by pushing or sweeping your hands out to meet them; if you do not field them clean you will often save a run by forcing the ball up towards the wicket-keeper, or having it before you.

A long stop wants much command of attention,—eye never off the ball; and this, so little thought of, is the great secret of all fielding: also to play your hardest and your very best; a habit which few men have energy to sustain. If you miss a ball, rattle away after it; do not stand, as many do, to apologize by dumb show. If the ball bumps up at the moment of handling, throw your chin up and let it hit your chest as full as it may: this is Horace's advice.

"*Fortiaque adversis opponite pectora rebus.*"

Longstop should always back up on the On side, and must start at once to be in time. The attention he has to sustain is very trying to the eyes, especially in windy weather.

WICKET-KEEPER.—If not born with better ocular nerves than the average, I doubt whether any degree of practice would make a first-rate wicket-keeper. To place the hands, right or left, accurately, according to the pitch of the ball, and to take that ball, however fast, unbaulked by the bat or body of the player, is really very difficult. But what, if we add, how few, very few, can accomplish it!—taking the ball in spite of an unexpected bias or turn from the bat. Still, practice will do much where nature has done a little; but with modern bowling you want a man both "rough and ready." Mr. Jenner was the latter; so also are Messrs. Anson, Nicholson, and Ridding and Box; but Wenman was ready and rough too. He had fine working qualities, and could stand a deal of pounding, day after day: others have had a short life and a merry one, and more transient popularity. Chatterton fears no pace in bowling. Lockyer's name, also, stands very high, and the All England Eleven experienced in one match the merit of Tinling as wicket-keeper as well as bowler. We leave these three to emulate Wenman, especially in his everyday lasting and working qualities against fast bowling, for that is the difficulty. Wenman did not stand too near, so was better placed for catches. Moreover, Wenman had weight and power: a decided advantage, as, by fast bowling, you are shaken off your equilibrium. By the way, Burt an old wicket-keeper, was twenty stone, and Mr. Winterton, of Cambridge, not much less. This gives a great advantage over a player of the weight of Mr. Ridding: albeit, in the Players' Match, he stumped Hillyer off Mr. Followes's bowling, and that by a leg ball! Hammond was the great wicket-keeper of former days: but then the bowling was often Clarke's pace. Browne, of Brighton, and Osbaldestone put wicket-keepers to flight; but the race re-appeared in the finest ever seen for moderate pace—Mr. Jenner, famed not only for the neatest stumping, but the marvellous quantity of ground he could cover, serving, as a near point, leg and slip, as well as wicket-keeper. Box's powers—though he has always been a first-rate man—are rather limited to pace. " Have me to bowl," Lillywhite used to say, " Box to keep wicket, and Pilch to hit, and then you'll see Cricket;" for Box is best with Lillywhite. As to making mistakes as wicket-keeper, what mortal combination of flesh and blood can help it? One of the most experienced long stops, after many years at Lord's and in the country, says, in his experience to take one chance even out of three has proved good average wicket-keeping; for think of leg-shooters, though Mr. Ridding takes even them wonderfully well.

"I have seen," writes Mr. E. S. E. H., " Mr. C. Taylor—who was capital at running in, and rarely stumped out, having an excellent eye, and if the twist of the ball beat him, it was enough to beat the wicket-keeper also—I have seen him, after missing a ball, walk quietly back to his ground, poor wicket-keeper looking foolish and vexed at not stumping him, and the ring, of course, calling him a muff." Really wicket-keepers are hardly used; the spectators little know that a twist that misses the bat may as easily escape the hand.

Again, " the best piece of stumping I ever saw was done by Mr. Anson, in the Players' Match, in 1845. Butler, one of the finest of the Nottingham batsmen, in drawing one of Mr. Mynn's leg shooters, just lifted, for an instant, his right foot ; Mr. Anson timed the feat beautifully, and swept the ball with his left hand into the wicket. I fancy a feat so difficult was never done so easily." " I also saw Mr. Anson, in a match against the Etonians, stump a man with his right, catch the flying bail with his left, and replace it so quickly that the man's surprise and puzzle made all the fun : stumped out, though wicket seemingly never down ! Mr. Jenner was very clever in these things, skimming off one bail with his little finger, ball in hand, and not troubling the umpire. Once his friend, Mr. R. K., had an awkward trick of pulling up his trousers, which lifted his leg every time he had missed a ball : Mr. Jenner waited for his accustomed habit, caught him in the act, and stumped him. A similar piece of fun happened in Gentlemen of England *v.* Gentlemen of Kent, in 1844." " A Kent player sat down to get wind after a run, his bat in his ground, but his seat of honor out, and for a moment let go the handle, and wicket-keeper stumped him out. He was very angry, and said he never would play again : however, he did play the return match at Canterbury, where he was put out in precisely the same manner. Since which, like Monsieur Tonson, he has never been heard of more."

That a fieldsman wants wits to his fingers' ends, was shown by Martingell one day: being just too far to command a ball, he gave it a touch to keep up, and cried, " Catch it, Slip." Slip, so assisted, reached the ball.

The great thing in wicket-keeping is, for hand and eye to go together, just as with batting, and what is exercise for the former, assists the latter. Any exercise, in which the hand habitually tries to obey the eye, is useful for cricket; fielding acts on batting, and batting on fielding. A batsman had better practise wicket-keeping, or long-stopping, alternately with batting, than batting alone.

" How do you explain, sir," said Cobbett, one day, standing with other professionals at Lord's, " that the player's batting keeps pace with the gentleman's, when we never take a bat except in a game?" " Because you are constantly following the ball with hand and eye together, which forms a valuable practice for judging pace, and time, and distance: not enough, certainly, to teach batting, but enough to keep it up. Besides, if you practise too little,—most gentlemen practise too much, ending in a kind of experimenting and speculative play,—that proves, like gentleman's farming, more scientific than profitable. They often try at too much, mix different styles, and, worse than all, *form conflicting habits.* The game, for an average, is the player's game, because less ambitious, with less excitement about favorite hits, simple style, with fewer things to think of, and a game in which, though limited, they are better grounded.

Amateurs are apt to try a bigger game than they could safely play with twice their practice. Many a man, for instance, whose talent lies in defence, tries free hitting, and between the two proves good for nothing. Others, perhaps, can play straight and fairly off; and should not they learn to hit on, also? Certainly; but, while in a transition state, they are not fit for the players' match: and some men are always in a transition state. There is more orthodoxy—that is, more of "Father's doxy"—in a young Caldecourt than in a young Etonian, and low-cricket notions of " private judgment" "lead many all abroad." Horace had good cricket ideas, for, said he,

"*Aut famam sequere aut sibi convenientia finge,*"

either play for shew off, or adopt a style you can put well together—and *sumite materiam—æquam viribus*. You won't win by a hitting game if there is no hit in you. But *cui lecta potenter erit res ;* try at no more than you can do,—*nec deseret hunc*,—and that's the game to carry you through.

A mistake, said an experienced bowler, in giving a leg ball or two, is not all dead loss ; for a swing round to the leg often takes a man off his straight play. To ring the changes on cutting with horizontal bat, forward play with a straight bat, and leg hitting, which takes a different bat again, requires far more steady practice than most who attempt it have either time or perseverance to learn so thoroughly as to prevent one movement from taking the place of the other.

## CHAP. XI.

#### CHAPTER OF ACCIDENTS.—MISCELLANEOUS.

LET any man of common judgment see the velocity with which the ball flies from the bats of first-rate players, and how near the fieldsmen stand to the hitter; and then let him feel and weigh a ball in his hand, and he would naturally expect to hear that every public cricket ground was in near connection with some casualty hospital, so deceptive is *à priori* reasoning. William Beldham saw as much of cricket as any other man in England, from the year 1780 to about 1820. Mr. E. H. Budd and Caldecourt are the best of chroniclers from the days of Beldham down to George Parr. Yet neither of these worthies could remember any injury at cricket, that would at all compare with the "moving accidents of flood and field" that have thinned the ranks of Nimrod, Hawker, or Isaac Walton. Fatal accidents in any legitimate game of cricket there have been none. There is a rumor of a boy at school, about fifteen years since, and another boy about twenty-five years ago, being severally killed by a blow on the head with a ball: a dirty boy, also, of Salisbury town, in 1826, having a bad habit of pocketing the balls of the pupils of Dr. Ratcliffe's school, was hit rather hard on the head with a brass-tipped middle stump, and, by a strange coincidence, died of "excess of passion," as the jury found a few hours after. A man fell over the stumps but a short time since, and died of the injury sustained in the leg. But all this proves little as to the danger of the game.

The most likely source of serious injury, and one which has caused alarm and shaken the nerves of not a few, is when a hitter, which is most rare, returns the ball, with all his force, straight back to the bowler. Caldecourt and the Rev. C. Wordsworth, than whom a more free and forcible hitter to every point of the field was never bred at Harrow, nor played at Winchester, severally and separately remarked in my hearing that they had shuddered at cricket once, each in the same position, and each from the same hitter. Each had a ball hit back to him by that powerful hitter, Colonel Kingscote, which whizzed, in defiance of hand or eye, most dangerously by. A similar hit we described from Hammond stepping in at the pitch, just missed Lord F. Beauclerk's head, and spoiled his nerve for bowling ever after. But what if these several balls had really hit? who knows whether the skull might not have stood the shock, as in a case which I witnessed in Oxford, in 1835; when one Richard Blucher, a Cowley bowler, was hit on the head by a clean half volley, from the bat of Henry Daubeney—than whom few Wykehamists *used* (*fuit!*) to hit with better eye or stronger arm. Still "Richard was himself again," for we saw a man, with his head tied up, bowling at shillings the very next day. Some skulls stand a great deal. Witness the sprigs of Shillelah in Donybrooke fair; still most indubitably tender is the face: as also—which *horresco referens*; but here let me tell wicket-keepers, and longstops especially, that a cricket-jacket, made long and full, with pockets to hold a handkerchief sufficiently in front, is a precaution not to be despised, though "the race of inventive men" have also devised a cross-bar India rubber guard, aptly described in Achilles' threat to Thersites, in the first Iliad; though I can truly say, like Bob Acres, at the sight of the doctor's implements, the sight of them "takes away my fighting stomach."

The most alarming accident I ever saw occurred in one of the many matches played by the Lansdown Club against Mr. E. H. Budd's Eleven, at Purton, in 1835. Two of the Lansdown players were running between wickets; and good Mr. Prout—*immani corpore*—was standing mid way, and hiding each from the other. Both rushing the same side of him, and one with his bat most dangerously extended, the point of which met his partner under the chin, forced back his head as if his neck were broken, and dashed him senseless to the ground. Never shall I forget the shudder and the chill of every heart, till poor Price—for he it was—was lifted up—gradually evinced returning consciousness; and, at length, when all was explained, he smiled, amidst his bewilderment, with his usual good-nature, on his unlucky friend. A surgeon, who witnessed the collision, feared he was dead, and said, afterwards, that with less powerful muscles (for he had a neck like a bulldog) he never could have stood the shock. Price told me next day that he felt as if a little more, and he never should have raised his head again.

And what Wykehamist of 1820–30 does not remember R—— Price? or what Fellow of New College down to 1847, when

"*Multis ille bonis flebilis occidit,*"

has not enjoyed his merriment in the Common Room, or his play on Bullingdon and Cowley Marsh? His were the safest hands and most effective fielding ever seen. To attempt the one run from a cover hit when Price was there, or to give the sight of one stump to shy at, was a wicket lost. When his friend, F. B. Wright, or any one he could trust, was at the wicket, well backed up, the ball by the fine old Wykehamist action was up and in with such speed and precision as I have hardly seen equalled, and never exceded. When he came to Lord's, in 1825, with that Wykehamist Eleven which Mr. Ward so long remembered with delight, their play was unknown, and the bets on their opponents; but when once Price was seen practising at a single stump, his Eleven became the favorites immediately; for he was one of the straightest of all fast bowlers; and I have heard experienced batsmen say, ' We don't care for his underhand bowling, only it is so straight we could take no liberties, and the first we missed was Out.' I never envied any man his sight and nerve like Price—the coolest practitioner you ever saw; he always looked bright, though others blue: you had only to look at his sharp gray eyes, and you could at once account for the fact that one stump to shy at, a rook for a single bullet, or the ripple of a trout in a bushy stream, was so much fun for R. Price.

Some of the most painful accidents have been of the same kind—from collision; therefore I never blame a man who, as the ball soars high in air, and the captain of his side does not (as he ought if he can) call out "Johnson has it!" stops short, for fear of three spikes in his instep, or the buttons of his neighbor's jacket forcibly coinciding with his own. Still these are hardly the dangers of cricket: men may run their heads together in the street.

The principal injuries sustained are in the fingers; though I did once know a gentleman who played in spectacles; and seeing two balls in the air, caught at the shadow, and nearly had the substance in his face. The old players, in the days of under-hand bowling, played without gloves; and Bennett assured me he had seen Tom Walker, before advancing civilization made man tender, rub his bleeding fingers in the dust. The old players could show finger-joints of most ungenteel dimensions; and no wonder, for a finger has been broken even through tubular India rubber. Still, with a good pair of cricket gloves no man need think much about his fingers; albeit flesh will blacken, joints will grow too large for the accustomed ring, and finger-nails will come off. A spinning ball is the most mischievous; and when there is spin and space too, as with a ball from Mr. Fellows, which you can hear humming like a top, the danger is too great for mere amusement; for when, as in the Players' Match of 1849, Hillyer plays a bowler a foot away from his stumps, and Pilch cannot face him, which is true when Mr. Fellows bowls on any but the smoothest ground, why then we will not say that any thing that hardest of hitters and thorough cricketers does is not cricket, but certainly it's anything but *play*.

Some of the worst injuries of the hands occur rather in fielding than in batting. A fine player of the Kent Eleven, about three years ago, so far injured his thumb that the middle joint was removed, and he has rarely played since. Another of the best players of his day broke a bone in his hand in putting down a wicket: but, strangest of all, I saw a Christchurch man at Oxford fielding Cover split up his hand an inch in length between his second and third fingers; but a celebrated university doctor of that day—yclept " *Mercurialium custos virorum* "—made all well in a few weeks, and in the same season a fine young fellow had a finger nail completely taken off in catching a ball.

Add to all these chances of war, the many balls that are flying at the same time at Lord's and the University, and other much frequented grounds, on a practising day. At Oxford, you may see, any day in the summer, on Cowley Marsh, two rows of six wickets each, facing each other, with a space of about sixty yards between each row, and ten between each wicket. Then you have twelve bowlers, *dos à dos*, and as many hitters—making twelve balls and twenty-four men, all in danger's way at once, besides bystanders. The most any one of these bowlers can do is to look out for the balls of his own set; whether hit or not by a ball from behind is very much a matter of chance. A ball from the opposite row once touched my hair. The wonder is, that twelve balls should be flying in a small space for nearly every day; yet I never heard of any man being hit in the face—a fact the more remarkable because there was usually free hitting and loose bowling. One day, at Lord's, just before the match bell rung after dinner, I saw one of the hardest hitters in the M. C. C. actually trying how hard he could drive among the various clusters of sixpenny amateurs, every man thinking it fun, and no one dangerous. Certainly, body-blows from a ball no man regards; and as to legs, the calves, as an Irishman remarked, save the shins behind, and the hands before. An elderly gentleman cannot stand a bruise so well—matter forms or bone exfoliates. But then, an elderly gentleman, bearing an inverse ratio in all things to him who calls him 'governor,' is the most careful thing in nature; while young blood circulates too fast to be overtaken by half the ills that flesh is heir to.

A well known Wykehamist player of R. Price's standing, was lately playing as wicket-keeper, and seeing the batsman going to hit off, ran almost to the place of a near Point; the hit, tremendously hard, glanced off from his forehead—he called out "Catch it," and it was caught by bowler! He was not hurt—not even marked by the ball.

Four was scored at Beckenham, 1850, by a hit that bounded off point's head; but the player suffered much in this instance.

A spot under the window of the tavern at Lord's was marked as the evidence of a famous hit by Mr. Budd, and when I played, Oxford v. Cambridge, in 1836, a son of Lord F. Beauclerk, hitting above that spot, elicited the observation from the old players. Beagley hit a ball from his Lordship over a bank 120 yards. Freemantle's famous hit was 130 yards in the air. Freemantle's bail was once hit up and fell back on the stump: Not out. A similar thing was witnessed by a friend on the Westminster Ground. "One hot day," said Bailey, "I saw a new stump bowled out of the perpendicular, but the bail stuck in the groove from the melting of the varnish in the sun, and the batsman continued his innings." I have seen Mr. Kirwan hit a bail thirty yards. A bail has flown forty yards.

I once chopped hard down upon a shooter, and the ball went a foot away from my bat straight forward towards the bowler, and then, by its rotary motion, returned in the same straight line exactly, like the "draw-back stroke" at billiards, and shook the bail off.

At a match played at Cambridge, a lost ball was found so firmly fixed on the point of a broken glass bottle in an ivied wall, that a new ball was necessary to continue the game.

Among remarkable games of cricket, are games on the ice—as on Christchurch meadow, Oxford, in 1849, and other places. The one-armed and one-legged pensioners of Greenwich and Chelsea is an oft-repeated match.

Mr. Trumper and his dog challenged and beat two players at single wicket in 1825, on Harefield common, near Rickmansworth.

Matches of much interest have been played between members of the same family and some other club. Besides "the Twelve Cæsars," the three Messrs.

Walker and the Messrs. Ridding have proved how cricket may run in a family, not to forget three of the House of Verulam, one of whom, especially, plays in as fine a style as any of the present day; and, as to hard hitting, a second has, I am informed, hit over the Tennis Court.

Pugilists have rarely been cricket players. "We used to see the fighting men," said Beldham, "playing skittles about the ground, but there were no players among them." Ned O'Neal was a pretty good player, and we did hear that Bendigo challenged George Parr; but no one imputed it to any distrust in his own play that Parr declined that honor. Certainly, no man was ever famous both in the ring and at Lord's.

In the famous Nottingham match, 1817, Bentley, on the All England side, was playing well, when he was given "run out," having run round his ground. "Why," said Beldham, "he had been home long enough to take a pinch of snuff." They changed the umpire; but the blunder lost the match.

"Spiked shoes," said Beldham, "were not in use in my country. Never saw them till I went to Hambledon." "Robinson began with spikes of a monstrous length," said old Mr. Moreton, the dramatist, on one foot. "The first notion of a leg guard I ever saw," said an old player, "was Robinson's: he put together two thin boards, angle-wise, on his right shin: the ball would go off it as clean as off the bat, but made a precious deal more noise: but it was laughed at — did not last long. Robinson burnt some of his fingers off when a child, and had the handle of his bat cut to suit the stumps. Still, he was a fine hitter.

Barton mentioned to me a one-armed man who used a short bat in his right hand so well as to make a fair average score.

SAWDUST. — Beldham, Robinson, and Lambert, played Bennett, Fennex, and Lord F. Beauclerk, a notable single wicket match at Lord's, 27th June, 1806. Lord Frederick's last innings was winning the game, and no chance of getting him out. His Lordship had then lately introduced sawdust when the ground was wet. Beldham, unseen, took up a lump of wet dirt and sawdust, and stuck it on the ball, which, pitching favorably, made an extraordinary twist, and took the wicket. This I heard separately from Beldham, Bennett, and also Fennex, who used to mention it as among the wonders of his long life.

As to LONG SCORES, above one hundred in an innings rather lessens than adds to the interest of a game.

The greatest number recorded, with overhand bowling, was in M. C. C. v. Sussex, at Brighton, about 1842; the four innings averaged 207 each. In 1815, Epsom v. Middlesex, at Lord's, scored first innings, 476. Sussex v. Epsom, in 1817, scored 445 in one innings. Mr. Ward's great innings was 278, in M. C.

C. v. Norfolk, 24th July, 1820, but with underhand bowling. Mr. Mynn's great innings at Leicester was in North v. South in 1836, South winning by 218 runs. Mr. Mynn 21 (not out) and 125 (not out) and against Redgate's bowling. Wisden, Parr, and Pilch, have scored above 100 runs in one innings against good bowling. Wisden once bowled ten wickets in one innings: Mr. Kirwan has done the same thing.

Mr. Marcon, at Beckenham, 1850, bowled four men in four successive balls. The Lansdown Club, in 1850, put the West Gloucestershire Club out for six runs, and of these only two were scored by hits—so ten ciphers! Eleven men last year (1850) were out for a run each, Mr. Felix being one. Mr. G. Yonge, playing against the Etonians, put a whole side out for six runs. A friend, playing the Shepton Mallet Club, put his adversaries in second innings for seven runs to tie, and got all out for five! In a famous Wykehamist match all depended on an outsider's making two runs: he made a hard hit. When in the moment of exultation, "Cut away, you young sinner," said a big fellow; when lo! down he laid his bat, and cut away to the tent; while the other side, amidst screams of laughter at the mistake, put down the wicket and won the match.

In a match at Oxford, in 1835, I saw the two last wickets score 110 runs; and in an I. Z. match at Leamington, the last wickets scored 80.

As to HARD HITTING. "One of the longest hits in air of modern days," writes a friend, "was made at Slimley about three years since by Mr. Fellows, confessedly one of the hardest of all hitters. The same gentleman, in practice on the Leicester ground, hit, clean over the poplars, one hundred long paces from the wicket: the distance from bat to pitch of ball may be fairly stated as 140 yards. This was a longer hit, I think, than that at Slimley, which every one wondered at, though the former was off slow lobs in practice; the latter in a match. Mr. Fellows also made so high a hit over the bowler's (Wisden's) head, that the second run was finished as the ball returned to earth! He was afterwards caught by Armitage, Long-field On, when half through the second run. I have also seen, I think, Mr. G. Barker, of Trinity, hit a nine on Parker's Piece. It took three average throwers to throw it up. Mr. Bastard, of Trinity, hit a ten on the same ground. Sir F. Heygate, this year, hit an eight at Leicester." When Mr. Budd hit a nine at Woolwich, it proved a tie match: an eighth would have lost the game. Practise clean hitting, correct position, and judgment of lengths with free arm, and the ball is sure to go far enough. The habit of hitting at a ball oscillating from a slanting pole will greatly improve any unpractised hitter. The drummer boys practise the use of the cat on a dummy. The use of the bat, by a kind of "chamber practice" mentioned, may furnish us an exercise as good as dumb bells, and, and far more interesting. A soft ball will answer the purpose, pierced and threaded on a string.

The most vexatious of all stupid things was done by James Broadbridge, in Sussex *v.* England, at Brighton, in 1827, one of the trial matches which excited such interest in the early days of overhand bowling. "We went in for 120 to win," said our good friend, Captain Cheslyn. "Now," I said, "my boys, let every man resolve on a steady game and the match is ours; when, almost at the first set off, that stupid fellow Jim threw his bat a couple of yards at a ball too wide to reach, and Mr. Ward caught him at point! The loss of this one man's innings was not all, for the men went in disgusted; the quicksilver was up with the other side, and down with us, and the match was lost by twenty-four runs." But, though stupid in this instance, Broadbridge was one of the most artful dodgers that ever handled a ball. And once he practised for some match till he appeared to all the bowlers about Lord's to have reduced batting to a certainty: but when the time came, amidst the most sanguine expectations of his friends, he made no runs.

Mr. A. Bass reminds me that I have said little about generalship, a point in which I well might profit by his long experience.

I agree with Mr. Bass that his old preceptor George

Owston's aim is of the greatest importance,—namely, to keep his man in good humor and good spirits.

The first thing the manager has to do is to choose his Eleven; and we have already hinted that fielding rather than batting is the qualification. A good field is sure to save runs, though the best batsman may not make any. When all are agreed on the bowlers, I would leave the bowlers to select such men as they can trust. Then in their secret conclave you will hear such principles of selection as these:—" King must be point, Chatterton we cannot afford to put cover unless you can ensure Wenman to keep wicket; Good must be longstop: his left hand saves so many draws; and I have not nerve to attack the leg stump as I ought to with any other man. We shall have three men at least against us whom we cannot reckon on bowling out; so if at the short slip we have a Hillyer, and at leg such a man as Coates of Sheffield, we may pick these men up pretty easily." " But as to Sir Wormwood Scrubbs, old Sloley vows he shall never get any more pine apples and champagne for the ladies' days if we don't have him, and he is about our sixth bat." " Can't be helped, for, what with his cigar and his bad temper, he will put us all wrong; besides, we must have John Gingerley, whose only fault is chaffing, and these two men will never do together: then for middle wicket we have Young George." " Why, Edwards is quite as safe." " Yes, but not half as tractable. I would never bowl without George if I could have him; his eye is always on me, and he will shift his place for every ball in the over, if I wish it. A handy man to put about in a moment just where you want him, is worth a great deal to a bowler."

" Then you leave out Kingsmill, Barker, and Cotesworth? Why, they can score better than most of the tail of the Eleven!"

" Yes; on practising days, with loose play, but, with good men against them, what difference can there be between two men, when the first ripping ball levels both alike?"

When taking the field, good humor and confidence, is the thing. A general who expects everything smooth, in dealing with ten fallible fellow creatures, should be at once dismissed the service: he must always have some man he had rather change, as Virgil says of the bees—

*Semper erunt quarum mutari corpora malis;*

but if you can have some four safe players,—

*Quatuor eximios præstanti corpore—*

join your influence with theirs, and lead them while you seem to consult them, and so keep up an appearance of working harmoniously together. Obviously two bowlers of different pace, like Clarke and Wisden, work well together, as also a left-handed and right-handed batsman, like Felix and Pilch, whom we have seen run up a hundred runs faster than ever before or since.

*Nunc dextrâ ingeminans ictus, nunc ille sinistrâ.*

Never put in all your best men at first, and leave "a tail" to follow: many a game has been lost in this manner, for men lose confidence when all the best are out: add to this most men play better for the encouragement that a good player often gives. And take care that you put good judges of a run in together. A good runner starts intuitively and by habit, where a bad judge, seeing no chance, hesitates and runs him out. If a good off hitter and a good leg hitter are in together, the same field that checks the one will give an opening to the other.

Frequent change of bowlers, where two men are making runs, is good: but do not change good bowling for inferior, till it is hit, unless you know your batsman is a dangerous man, only waiting till his eyes are open.

With a fine forward player, a near middle wicket or forward point often snaps up a catch, and is worth trying as the man comes in; otherwise, a third slip up can hardly be spared.

If your wicket-keeper is not likely to stump any one, make a slip of him, provided you play a short leg; otherwise he is wanted at the wicket for the single runs.

And if Point is no good as Point for a sharp catch, make a field of him. A bad Point will make more catches, and save more runs some yards back. Many a time have I seen both Point and wicket-keeper standing where they were by use. The general must place his men not on any plan or theory, but where each particular man's powers can be turned to the best account. We have already mentioned the common error of men standing too far to save one, and not as far as is compatible with saving two.

Bowlers are not always good judges of play: the general should observe how near the ball may be pitched to the batsmen respectively. Though, of course, it is a fatal error to worry the bowler by too many directions.

With a free hitter, a man who does not pitch very far up answers best: short leg balls are not easily hit. A lobbing bowler, with the longstop, and four men in all on the On side, will shorten the innings of many a reputed fine hitter.

If a man will not play forward, pitch well up to him, and depend upon your slips.

A good arrangement of your men, according to these principles, will make eleven men do the work of thirteen. Some men play nervously at first they come in, so it is so much waste of your forces to lay your men far out, and equally a waste not to open your field as they begin to hit.

We must conclude with comments on the Laws of the Game.

I. The ball must weigh not less than five ounces and a half, nor exceed five ounces and three-quarters. It must measure not less than nine inches in circumference, nor more than nine inches and one quarter. Either party may call for a new ball at the beginning of each innings.—

The secretaries of country clubs should order balls and cricket implements from the makers. Our friends may safely address Mr. Barton, Lord's, or 7 Connaught Terrace: he will judiciously select from the stores of Caldecourt, Dark, Lillywhite, and others, and send choice articles of every kind. A bad ball will spoil any bats, and puzzle the bowler with its false weight. We once were playing a match with Mr. Budd, when, at the first feel of the ball, he called out, " we cannot play with this—a stone ball bought at a toy-shop." Shortly after, such a ball cut a new bat like a lump of lead, and damaged hands in the same proportion. Before the days of John Small, a ball would not last a match, through the stitches giving way. To " call for a new ball at the beginning of each innings " is not customary now.

II. The bat must not be wider than four inches and a quarter in the widest part; nor more than thirty-eight inches in length.—

Here the length of the blade of the bat may be anything the player likes short of thirty-eight inches. As to the width, an iron frame was used in the old Hambledon Club as a gauge, in those primitive days when the Hampshire yeomen shaped out their own bats. This measure, we have said, was applied in the case of Robinson. As to the weight of the bat, 2 lb. 2 oz. is wood enough for a cutting and quick hitter; only, very light bats rarely last long; so, a good player must remember that it is the nature of bats to wear out.

III. The stumps must be three in number; twenty-seven inches above the ground; the bails eight inches in length; the stumps of equal and sufficient thickness to prevent the ball from passing through.

The wicket has been of different sizes at different times, as represented in the following woodcut. In the year 1700, the runner was made out, not by striking off the transverse stump—we can hardly call it a bail—but by popping the ball in the hole herein represented.

The measurement of the year 1817 is that now observed: at that time one inch was added to the height of the stumps, and two inches to the width between the creases.

IV. The bowling crease must be in a line with the stumps; six feet eight inches long; the stumps in the centre; with a return crease at each end at right angles towards the bowler.

V. The popping crease must be four feet from the wicket, and parallel to it: unlimited in length, but not shorter than the bowling crease,—

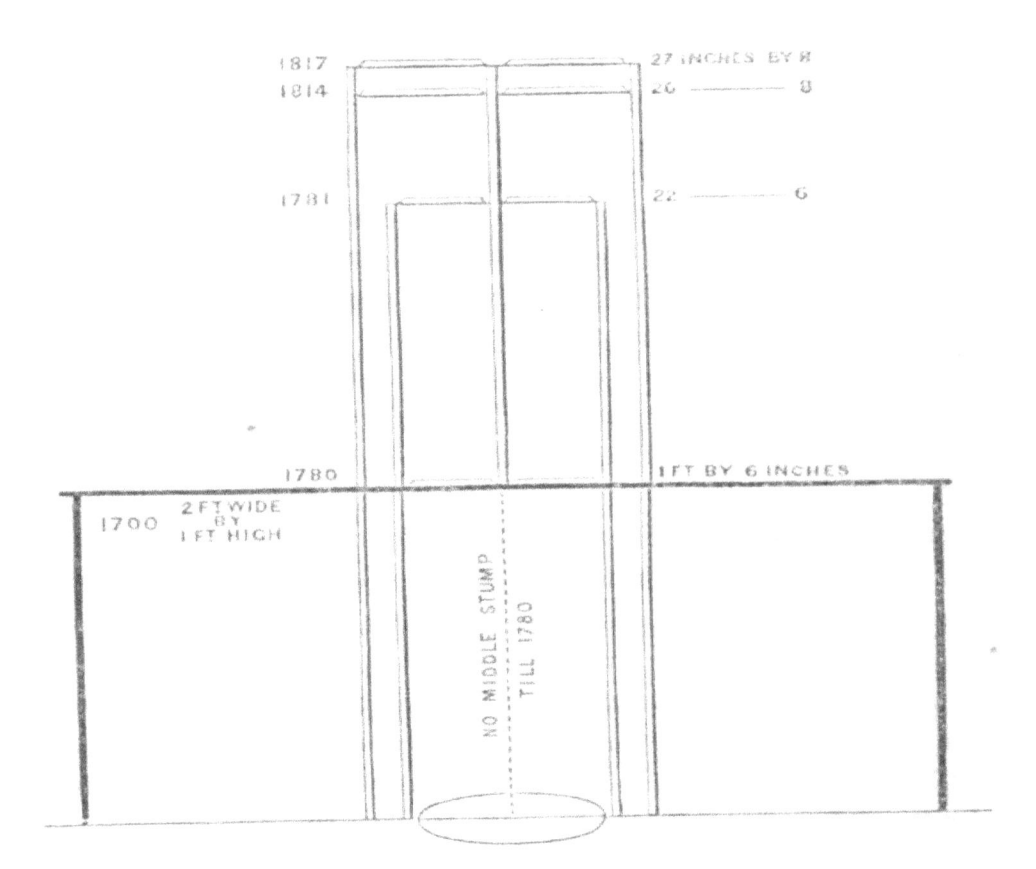

"Unlimited in length, but not shorter than the bowling crease." These words imply that the crease actually chalked out should be not shorter than the bowling crease, and *unlimited* in this sense, that it shall not be said the runner is out because he ran round his ground, for the popping crease is supposed to extend to the end of the field.

The reason the bowling crease is limited, is because, otherwise, the batsman never could take guard; and umpires should be very careful to call "No Ball," if the bowler bowls outside the return crease; otherwise the best of batsmen might, undeservedly, lose his innings.

The reason the return crease is not limited by law is, that it is against a batsman's own interest to run wide of his wicket: besides, a little latitude is requisite to prevent dangerous collision with the wicket-keeper.

VI. The wickets must be pitched opposite to each other, by the umpires, at the distance of twenty-two yards.

Secretaries should provide a rule or frame, consisting of two wooden measures, six feet eight inches long, and four feet apart, and perfectly parallel to each other. Then, if the chain of twenty-two yards be stretched from the extreme end of one bowling crease to the extreme end of the other, the wickets may easily be placed "opposite each other."

VII. It is not lawful for either party, during a match, without consent, to alter the ground by rolling, watering, mowing, or beating. This rule is not meant to prevent the striker from beating the ground with his bat near the spot where he stands during the innings; nor to prevent the bowler from filling up holes with sawdust, &c., when the ground is wet.

VIII. After rain, the wickets may be changed with the consent of both parties.

IX. The bowler shall deliver the ball with one foot on the ground behind the bowling crease, and within the return crease, and shall bowl four balls before he change wickets, which he shall be permitted to do once only in the same innings.

" One foot on the ground behind the return crease." Sometimes a dispute arises as to whether the foot, though admitted "behind," was actually "on the ground." This is a nice point for the eye to decide, because you cannot look at the foot and the hand at the same moment. But Clarke observed to us, that no man can deliver a ball with the foot not touching the ground in the full swing of bowling: and, from experiment, we believe he is right. So, if the foot is over the crease, there is no doubt of its being on the ground.

"Shall bowl four balls." When time is limited, it is not uncommon to agree on playing "six balls and over." Cobbett used to say, he could not take such pains for six balls as for four: it is usually found too fatiguing for fast bowlers.

X. The ball must be bowled, not thrown or jerked, and the hand must not be above the shoulder in delivery; and whenever the bowler shall so closely infringe on this rule in either of the above particulars as to make it difficult for the umpire at the bowler's wicket to judge whether the ball has been delivered within the true intent and meaning of this rule or not, the umpire shall call, "no ball."

"Not thrown or jerked:" here there is not a word about " touching the side with the arm," too commonly quoted as the criterion of a jerk. It is left to the umpire to decide what is a jerk. We once heard an umpire asked, how could you make out that to be a jerk? " I say it is a jerk because it is a jerk," was the sensible reply. "I know a jerk when I see one, and I have a right to believe my eyes, though I cannot define wherein a jerk consists."

In a jerk, there is a certain mechanical precision and curl of the ball wholly unlike fair bowling.

A throw may be made in two ways; one way with an arm nearly straight from first to last: this throw with straight arm requires the hand to be raised as high as the head, and brought down in a whirl or circle, the contrary foot being used as the pivot on which the body moves in the delivery. But the more common throw, under pretence of bowling, results from the hand being first bent on the fore-arm, and then power of delivery being gained by the sudden lash out and straightening of the elbow. It is a mistake to say that the action of the wrist makes a throw.

"The hand must not be above the shoulder in delivery." David Harris used, before starting to bowl, to hold the ball high over his head, as if to gain freedom of arm. This the rule is not designed to prevent: but to plead that the hand that had gained its power above the shoulder is not " above the shoulder in delivery," because it had descended below the shoulder by the time the ball left the hand, this does appear too nice a distinction to be allowed.

"In delivery" means some action so called: if the mere opening of the hand is delivery of the ball, then the only question is the height of the hand the moment it opens. But if, as we think, "delivery" comprehends the last action of the arm that gives such opening of the hand effect, then in no part of that action may the hand be above the shoulder.

Further, in case of doubt as to fair bowling, the umpire is to decide against the bowler; so the hand must be *clearly* not above the shoulder, and the ball as clearly not thrown, nor jerked.

Now, as to high delivery as a source of danger, we never yet witnessed that kind of high bowling that admitted of a dangerous increase of speed in an angry moment. The only bowling ever deemed dangerous, has been clearly below the shoulder, and savoring more of a jerk, or of an underhand sling, or throw, than of the round-armed or high delivery. Such bowlers were Mr. Osbaldestone, Browne, of Brighton, Mr. Kirwan, Mr. Fellowes, and Mr. Marcon, neither of whom, except on smooth ground, should we wish to encounter under the name of *play*.

Still a high delivery, though not conducing to a dangerous pace and unlimited power, is plainly contrary to the law as now explained.

But, we have often been asked, do the law and the practice coincide? Is it not a fact that few round-armed bowlers are clearly below the shoulder? Undoubtedly this is the fact. The better the bowler, as we have already explained, the more horizontal and the fairer his delivery. Cobbett and Hillyer have eminently exemplified this principle; but amongst amateurs and all but the most practised bowlers, allowing, of course, for some exceptions, the law is habitually infringed. In a country match a strict umpire would cry " no ball " to the bowlers on both sides, cramp their action, produce wide balls and loose bowling, and eventually, not to spoil the day's sport, the two parties would come to a compromise. And do such things ever happen? Not often. Because the umpires exercise a degree of discretion, and the law in the country is often a dead letter. Practically, the 10th law enables a fair umpire to prevent an undisguised and dangerous throw; but, at the same time, it enables an unfair umpire to put aside some promising player who is as fair as his neighbor's, but has not the same clique to support him.

What, then, would we suggest? The difficulty is in the nature of the case. To leave all to the umpire's discretion would, as to fair bowling, increase those evils of partiality, and, instead of an uncertain standard, we should have no standard at all. With fair umpires the law does as well as many other laws as it is; with unfair umpires no form of words would mend the matter. I can never forget a remark of the late Mr. Ward:—" Cricketers are a very peaceably disposed set of men. We play for the love of play; the fairer the play the better we like it. Otherwise, so indefinite is the nature of round-arm bowling, that I never yet saw a match about which the discontented might not find a pretext for a wrangle."

XI. He may require the striker at the wicket from which he is bowling to stand on that side of it which he may direct.

Query. Can a bowler give guard for one side of the wicket and bowl the other? No law (though law XXXVI. may apply) plainly forbids it; still, no gentleman would ever play with such a bowler another time.

XII. If the bowler shall toss the ball over the striker's head, or bowl it so wide that, in the opinion of the umpire, it shall not be fairly within the reach of the batsman, he shall adjudge one run to the parties receiving the innings, either with or without an appeal, which shall be put down to the score of wide balls: such ball shall not be reckoned as one of the four balls; but, if the batsman shall by any means bring himself within the reach of the ball, the run shall not be adjudged.

As to wide balls, some think there should be a mark making the same ball wider to a man of six feet and to a man of five. With good umpires, the law is better as it is. Still, any parties can agree on a mark for wide balls, if they please, before they begin the game.

"Bowl it so wide." These words say nothing about the ball pitching more or less straight and turning off afterwards: the distance of the ball when it passes the batsman is the point at issue.

XIII. If the bowler deliver a *no ball* or a *wide ball*, the striker shall be allowed as many runs as he can get, and he shall not be put out except by running out. In the event of no run being obtained by any other means, then one run shall be added to the score of *no balls* or *wide balls*, as the case may be. All runs obtained for *wide balls* to be scored to *wide balls*. The names of the bowlers who bowl *wide balls* or *no balls* in future to be placed on the score, to show the parties of whose bowling either score is made.

XIV. At the beginning of each innings the umpire shall call "play;" from that time to the end of each innings no trial ball shall be allowed to any bowler.

XV. The striker is out if either of the bails be bowled off, or if a stump be bowled out of the ground.

XVI. Or, if the ball from the stroke of the bat, or hand, but not the wrist, be held before it touch the ground, although it be hugged to the body of the catcher.

"Be held before it touch the ground." Query, is a ball caught rolling back off the tent out? If the ball striking the tent is, by agreement, so many runs, then the ball is dead, and a man cannot therefore be out. Otherwise, I should reason that the tent, being on the ground, is as part of the ground. By the spirit of the law it is *not out,* by the letter *out.* But, to avoid the question, the better plan would be not to catch the ball, and disdain to win a match except by good play.

XVII. Or, if in striking, or at any other time while the ball shall be in play, both his feet shall be over the popping crease, and his wicket put down, except his bat be grounded within it.

XVIII. Or, if in striking at the ball, he hit down his wicket.—

"In striking," not in running a notch, however awkwardly.

XIX. Or, if under pretence of running, or otherwise, either of the strikers prevent a ball from being caught, the striker of the ball is out,—

"Or otherwise;" as, for instance, by calling out purposely to baulk the catcher.

XX. Or, if the ball be struck, and he wilfully strike it again.—

"Wilfully strike it again." This obviously means, when a man blocks a ball, and afterwards hits it away to make runs. A man may hit a ball out of his wicket, or block it hard. The umpire is sole judge of the striker's intention, whether to score or to guard.

This law was, in one memorable instance, applied to

the case of one Smith, a fine Nottingham player, who, in the match mentioned in page 88, as he was running a notch, hit the ball, to prevent it coming home to the wicket-keeper's hands. Clarke, who was then playing, thinks the player was properly given out. Certainly he deserved to be out; but old laws do not always fit new offences, however flagrant.

XXI. Or, if in running, the wicket be struck down by a throw, or by the hand or arm (with ball in hand), before his bat (in hand) or some part of his person be grounded over the popping-crease. But if both the bails be off, a stump must be struck out of the ground."

"With ball in hand." The same hand.

"Bat (in hand);" that is, not thrown.

XXIII. Or, if the striker touch, or take up the ball while in play, unless at the request of the opposite party.

"If the striker touch." This applies to the Nottingham case better than Law XX.; but neither of these laws contemplated the exact offence. Last season a ball ran up a man's bat, and spun into the pocket of his jacket; and, as he "touched" the ball to get it out of his pocket, was given out. The reply of Mr. Bell on the subject was, the player was out for touching the ball—he might have shaken it out of his pocket. This we mention for the curiosity of the occurrence.

XXIV. Or, if with any part of his person he stop the ball, which, in the opinion of the umpire at the bowler's wicket, shall have been pitched in a straight line from it to the striker's wicket, and would have hit it.

"With any part of his person." A man has been properly given out by stopping a ball with his arm below the elbow. Also a short man, who stooped to let the ball pass over his head, and was hit in the face, was once given out, as before wicket.

"From it;" that is, the ball must pitch in a line, not from the hand, but from wicket to wicket.

Much has been said on this law.

Clarke and others say that a round arm bowler can rarely hit the wicket at all with a ball not over-pitched, unless it pitch out of the line of the wickets. If this is true, a ball that has been pitched straight " would *not* have hit it;" and a ball that " would have hit it," could not have been " pitched straight;" and therefore it is argued the condition " in a straight line from it (the wicket)" should be altered to " in a straight line from the bowler's hand." In support of this theory, others have drawn a line from a round arm bowler's hand to off-stump; and, observe, that the point in which that line enters into the line from wicket to wicket is too near for the pitch of a good ball.

On the other hand, some scientific observers having their attention specially directed to this very question, say that it is a matter of positive experience, that a round-arm bowler may pitch in the line of the wicket good length balls, and hit the wicket; and infer that, therefore, the law is sound.

The objection to adopting the line of the bowler's hand instead of the line of the wicket, is, that the umpire can actually see in the latter case, but in the former must guess.

And what do we say?

Bring the matter to an issue thus: stretch a thin white string from leg-stump of striker's to off-stump of the bowler's wicket; and let the facts carefully observed be the basis of future theories. The fact should be placed beyond all doubt; some umpires give glaring cases of leg before wicket Not Out, in support of a theory that has been promulgated, that the two conditions of the law ("straight pitch," and " would have hit") cannot possibly be fulfilled. That they are sometimes fulfilled we have no doubt: whether they are fulfilled as the rule, or only as the exception (as by a "break"), an experiment must decide.

The following points have suggested many a reference to Mr. Bell:

1. Whether a man is out when his partner strikes a ball through his wicket, he being out of the ground?— Not unless the ball touched the hand of one of the opposite party.

2. Whether a ball hitting a tent or building, and bounding back into a player's hand, is a fair catch?—

Supposing a hit to the tent is allowed to be a certain score, without running, the ball touching it is dead, and cannot make a man out. Otherwise, *me judice*, touching the ground, or anything on the ground, is the same thing. The better plan is not to catch the ball, nor raise the question, but win by play instead of chance.

Nothing is so unlike a good or fair player as to be continually asking questions of the umpire.

One of the fairest retorts I ever heard was this:

"How 's that, umpire?"

"Sir! you know it is not out: so why ask me, if you mean fair play?"

## "A LITTLE LEARNING IS A DANGEROUS THING" IN CRICKET.

The only piece of science I ever hear on a cricket field is this: "Sir, how can that be? The angle of reflection must always be equal to the angle of incidence."

That a cricketer should have only one bit of science, and that, as he applies it, a blunder, is indeed a pity.

I have already shown that, in bowling, the *apparent* angle of reflection is rendered unequal to the angle of incidence by the rotatory motion or spin of the ball, and also by the roughness of the ground.

I have now to explain that this law is equally disturbed in batting also; and by attention to the following observations, many a forward player may learn so to adapt his force to the inclination of his bat as not to be caught out, even although (as often happens to a man's great surprise) he plays over the ball!

Ask, my friends, some Cantab to tell you a little about the composition and resolution of forces. Any senior opt. (within a year after he has taken his degree) will inform you that the effect of a moving body meeting another body moving, and that same body quiescent, is rather different. So —

Fix a bat *immovably* perpendicular in the ground, and suppose a ball rises to it from the ground in an angle of 45° as the angle of incidence; then supposing the ball to have no rotatory motion, it will be reflected at an equal angle.

But supposing the bat is not fixed, but brought forcibly forward to meet the ball, then, according to the weight and force of the bat, the natural direction of the ball will be annihilated, and the ball returned, perhaps nearly point-blank, not in the line of reflection but in some other line more nearly resembling the line in which the bat is moved.

If the bat were at rest, or only played very gently forward, the angles of reflection would not be materially disturbed, but the ball would return to the ground in proportion nearly as it rose from it; but by playing very hard forward, the batsman annihilates the natural downward tendency of the ball, and drives it forward, perhaps, into the bowler's hands; and then, fancying the laws of gravitation have been suspended to spite him, he walks back disgusted to the pavilion, and says, "No man in England could help being out then. I was as clean over the ball as I could be, and yet it went away as a catch!"

Lastly, as to "being out by luck," always consider whether, with the same adversaries, Pilch or Parr would have been so put out. Our opinion is, that could you combine the experience and science of Pilch with the hand and eye of Parr, luck would be reduced to an infinitesimal quantity.

That cricket is partly a game of chance there can be no doubt; but that all is chance that men call such, we strenuously deny. Young players should not think of being out by chance: there is a certain intuitive adaptation of play to circumstances, that, however seemingly impossible, will result from observation and experience, unless the idea of chance closes the eyes to instruction.

With these hints, we bid our brother cricketers adieu; assuring them that we are ourselves by no means too old to learn; that all information will be thankfully received; and requesting, in the words of Horace,—

——— "si quid novisti rectius istis
Candidus imperti; si non, his utere mecum."

THE END.

**Uniform with Base Ball Player's Companion.**

# THE

# CRICKET PLAYER'S

## POCKET COMPANION.

CONTAINING

**PLANS FOR LAYING OUT THE GROUNDS,**

FORMING CLUBS, &c., &c.,

TO WHICH ARE ADDED

RULES AND REGULATIONS FOR CRICKET,

ADOPTED BY THE

MARY-LE-BONE CLUB.

BOSTON:
MAYHEW & BAKER, 208 WASHINGTON STREET.
1859.

Uniform with Cricket Player's Companion.

# THE
# BASE BALL PLAYER'S
# Pocket Companion.

CONTAINING

RULES AND REGULATIONS FOR FORMING CLUBS,

DIRECTIONS FOR PLAYING THE

"MASSACHUSETTS GAME,"

AND THE

"NEW YORK GAME,"

FROM OFFICIAL REPORTS.

ILLUSTRATED, CLOTH.

BOSTON:
MAYHEW & BAKER, 208 WASHINGTON STREET.
1859.

THE THROWER.

[Base Ball Player's Pocket Companion.]

THE STRIKER.

[Base Ball Player's Pocket Companion.]

**THE CATCHER.**

[Base Ball Player's Pocket Companion.]

**BASE TENDER.**

[Base Ball Player's Pocket Companion.]

# JUVENILE PUBLICATIONS
## OF
# MAYHEW & BAKER,

Publishers, Booksellers, and Stationers,

208 WASHINGTON ST., BOSTON.

# THE SEA OF ICE,
## OR THE
# ARCTIC ADVENTURERS.

**WITH NEW AND ELEGANT ILLUSTRATIONS.**

Price, 75 cents.

This is the Story of a young Englishman who sailed to discover the Northwest Passage, in search of which Sir John Franklin lost his life. By the mutiny of his crew, he was left upon the ice. The narrative gives his adventures, together with those of a faithful servant, who found means to join him. The whole book is a succession of stirring adventures and narrow escapes.

**Mayhew & Baker's Publications.**

# WILLIS THE PILOT,

### A SEQUEL TO THE

### SWISS FAMILY ROBINSON,

Being the further Adventures of an

### EMIGRANT FAMILY ON A DESERT ISLAND,

Interspersed with

### Tales, Incidents of Travel, and Illustrations of Natural History.

Price, 75 cents.

Of all the numerous books published for children, we know of no one which has in so short a time become such a favorite. It is beautifully Illustrated, handsomely bound, and worthy a place in the library of all young people.

## Mayhew & Baker's Publications.

ALICE LEARMONT, OR A MOTHER'S LOVE. By Miss Muloch, author of "John Halifax." A new Illustrated Holiday Edition, containing all the illustrations of the London edition, never before published in this country.

We have already sold two editions of this delightful Fairy Tale with part of the illustrations; we now present it fully illustrated. No one should fail to read this delightful tale of a mother's love. New edition. Price, 75 cents.

THE KING OF THE GOLDEN RIVER, OR THE BLACK BROTHERS. By the celebrated John Ruskin. With 22 Illustrations, beautifully printed and elegantly bound.
[Nearly ready.] Price, 75 cents.

KING JOLLYBOY'S ROYAL STORY BOOK. A large quarto Juvenile, printed in colors, with colored cover of new and unique design. Third edition. Price, 38 cents.

THE FIRESIDE PICTURE ALPHABET OF HUMOR AND DROLL MORAL TALES. Small quarto, printed in colors.
Price, 25 cents.

#### Mayhew & Baker's Publications.

## FIRESIDE PICTURE BOOKS.

**THE HISTORY OF THE LITTLE MAN AND HIS LITTLE GUN.** From Mother Goose. Illustrated.

**THE ROBBER KITTEN.** By the Author of "Three Little Kittens." Illustrated.

**THE HEADLONG CAREER AND WOFUL ENDING OF PRECOCIOUS PIGGY.** By the late Thomas Hood. Illustrated.

All the above are new, well printed, in large type and handsome covers.

Price, plain, 12 cents; colored, 25 cents.

## BLOCK ALPHABETS.

**THE LITTLE PET'S SCARLET ALPHABET BLOCKS.** Printed in colors on blocks two inches square, and packed in a handsome box.

Blocks and box, nicely varnished, price, $1.25.

They are the handsomest set of blocks made in this conntry.

## Mayhew & Baker's Publications.

**THE LITTLE PET'S SCARLET ALPHABET CARDS.** Printing and varnishing same as the blocks, but pasted on thick cards. Packed in handsome box. Price, 50 cents.

# NEW AND AMUSING GAMES.

**THE GAME OF YANKEE LAND.** A New Game on the History of our Country, combining amusement and instruction. The Battle of Bunker Hill, Death of General Warren, Throwing the Tea Overboard, and other scenes of the American Revolution, are represented in colors. Price, 38 cents.

**THE GAME OF SCHOOL IN AN UPROAR.** A pleasing pastime for children, will amuse all, and offend none. Price, 38 cents.

**THE GAME OF THE GIPSEY FORTUNE-TELLER.** A new and delightful method of describing future as well as present events. Price, 38 cents.

### Mayhew & Baker's Publications.

**THE DISSECTED GAME OF COMICAL DOMINOES.** One of the most agreeable pastimes for children. By these Cards more than 100 comical heads can be formed. In fact, there is no end to the changes of countenances which can be made by these "Helps to the Nursery." Price, 38 cents.

**THE GAME OF THE YOUNG PEDLERS, OR LEARNING TO COUNT IN A PLEASANT MANNER.** Instructive and amusing. Price, 38 cents.

**JACK AT ALL TRADES, OR HOME AMUSEMENTS FOR WINTER EVENINGS.** A collection of Toys printed on pasteboard, to be cut out and put together. Price, 38 cents.

The above Six Games are on cards, in boxes, size four by six inches. Cards and boxes colored in handsome style. Those in search of new games will do well to look at them.

**THE NEW GAMES OF TOURNAMENT AND KNIGHTHOOD,** combined on one board. An elegant and favorite game. Second Edition. Now ready. Price, 75 cents.

## Mayhew & Baker's Publications.

### THE GAME OF PLUM PUDDING.
By the Author of "Three Little Kittens." An amusing game. Price, 25 cents.

## RECENT PUBLICATIONS.

### COUNTERPARTS, OR THE CROSS OF LOVE.
By the Author of "Charles Auchester." Fifth Edition. Now ready.
Price, cloth, $1.00 : paper, 50 cents.

### PROVERBIAL & MORAL THOUGHTS,
In a Series of Essays, by Charles Henry Hanger.

"Let virtue, goodness, truth,
Be thy first, thy earliest aim."

These Essays are carefully and thoughtfully written. Price, 63 cents.

### THE CRICKET FIELD.
The Text-Book of England for that favorite game. 15 Illustrations. Price, $1.00.

## Mayhew & Baker's Publications.

**THE CRICKET PLAYER'S POCKET COMPANION.** Containing the Rules for Cricket. Price, 25 cents.

**THE BASE-BALL PLAYER'S POCKET COMPANION.** A Complete Manual of Base-Ball. Price, 25 cents.

**THE POCKET SCHOOLMASTER.** Errors in Speaking and Writing Corrected, with a few words on letters H and R; familiar synonymes and words of similar sound distinguished. Flexible cloth. Price, 25 cents.

For sale by all booksellers, or sent by mail on receipt of price. Address

**MAYHEW & BAKER,**

208 Washington St., Boston.

OCT 7 1879
SEP 18 1880
1 1880
DEC 19 1884
APR 25 1885
MAY 12 1887
OCT 17 1887
MAY 1888
MAR 1890
1904

CANCELLED
NOV 4 - 1985
NOV 7 - 1985

DUE APR 25 '47

Check Out More Titles From HardPress Classics Series In this collection we are offering thousands of classic and hard to find books. This series spans a vast array of subjects – so you are bound to find something of interest to enjoy reading and learning about.

Subjects:
Architecture
Art
Biography & Autobiography
Body, Mind &Spirit
Children & Young Adult
Dramas
Education
Fiction
History
Language Arts & Disciplines
Law
Literary Collections
Music
Poetry
Psychology
Science
…and many more.

Visit us at www.hardpress.net

# Im The Story
*personalised classic books*

**UNIQUE GIFT**
FOR KIDS, PARTNERS AND FRIENDS

## Timeless books such as:

### Kids

Alice in Wonderland • The Jungle Book • The Wonderful Wizard of Oz
Peter and Wendy • Robin Hood • The Prince and the Pauper
The Railway Children • Treasure Island • A Christmas Carol

### Adults

Romeo and Juliet • Dracula

- **Highly Customizable**
- **Change Book Title**
- **Replace Character Names**
- **Upload Photo for Front Page**
- **Add Inscriptions**

Visit **ImTheStory.com**
*and order yours today!*